YOUR TIME IS NOW!

The Millionaire Mindset

BY MARC PELLETZ

(One of the most successful investors of our time)

Copyright © 2019 by Marc Pelletz

All rights reserved. No part of this publication may be reproduced, distributed, or transmitted in any form or by any means, including photocopying, recording, or other electronic or mechanical methods, without the prior written permission of the publisher, except in the case of brief quotations embodied in critical reviews and certain other noncommercial uses permitted by copyright law.

TABLE OF CONTENTS

Foreword 1
About The Author 3
From The Author 4
Introduction 6

PART 1 - THINK LIKE AN INVESTOR 11

   Desire 13
   Decision 15
      Think It. Feel It. Achieve It 16
   Thoughts 18
   The Importance Of Gratitude 20
   Faith 22
   Goals 25
   Specialized Knowledge 28
   Building Your Team 33
   Gratitude 36
   Investments: Stand Alone Properties 39
   Giving Back 41
   Habits - Putting It All Together 43
   Summary 46

PART 2 – TIME TO MASTER THE GAME OF LIFE 49

   Not Again (Or, Why Me?) 51
   I Started With Nothing And Built A Fortune, More Than Once 55
   Your Destination 63
   The Real Estate Business In A Nutshell 64

It Is Time To Find Your Niche. Let's Start Now. 64

Why Real Estate? 65
In The Niches We Get Riches 67
    Choosing Your Path Is About Getting To Know Yourself First
    And Foremost. 67

Niches 68
    How Does Real Estate Build Your Wealth? 68
    How To Start Without Money 70
    Taking Over Existing Financing 78

Other Important Decisions You Must Make 79
    Choosing Location 79
    Hard Money – Paying For Convenience 84
    Positioning For Safety 88
    It's Important To Know That Real Estate Is Only A Tool. 89
    Financial Freedom 90
    What Your Real Estate Business Plan Should Include 91
    How To Get Started With Little Or No Money – Yes, You Can
    Do This! 94
    Building A Team To Succeed 96
    You're Going To Need A Good Management Team, As Well. . 100
    Finding Opportunity 108
    One Crucial Question: Where Are All The Rich People? 113

**PART 3 – HOW YOU LIVE YOUR LIFE (B) THE LONGER
VERSION** 115

The Keys To Freedom And Success 117
    Learning How To Learn To Be Effective 117

What Is The Real Meaning Of Power? 125

Replacing Old Conditioning With New, Chosen Conditioning. Becoming The Programmer 126

Build The New You Now. 132

The Key To Transformation: Start The Day 135

    How My Life Changed After I Learned How To Start Each Day 141

How You Live Your Life.. 148

    The Strength You Get From Taking Control Of Your Life. 154

The New You 166

    The Most Important And Valuable Part, So Far, Of Your New Journey: 166

Some Quantum Musings.. 168

The basics of creating a life of your dreams are outlined in Part 1 of this book.

I hope you find it helpful and use it as a guide on your journey to becoming the best you.

INTRODUCTION

Transformation. This book has a modest goal: to change your life. It begins as a book about real estate investing but investing in real estate is just a tool. It is the tool I've used to leverage my desire and will into a substantial business empire, more than once, as I will explain in more detail further on.

Real estate is the touchstone of this book not because the lessons I've derived from it are special or unique. In fact, that's the real point – real estate is what I can use to talk about the things I can impart because it's the road I've traveled. The means to achieve that success are essentially the same, regardless of what business you want to talk about.

More significantly, these are the same methods you can use to manifest whatever you set your sights on and succeed, whether the definition of success that you choose is financial well-being, becoming a respected and influential member of your community, of any other personal goals you set for yourself.

The wheres and hows of how I built my real estate business are laid out here as a template for you. I've tried to tell you my story with enough information to give you a head start in figuring out what kind of real estate business might light a fire inside you. Toward that end, I have tried to sketch out a brief outline of different approaches to starting and growing your own business, from low- or no-money-down deals to compiling a portfolio of investment and income properties in your own town or branching out to new markets and speculative investing. I have also tried to suggest some specific places to go to get started in searching for and finding the kinds of deals I have described.

My goals in doing that are modest. I am not trying to offer a comprehensive guide to one or another type of real estate investment. The truth is, there are already plenty of good books about that and I do not need to spend my time trying to duplicate or outdo them. Nor am I convinced that the world really needs one more such book. This is not a vanity project.

The lessons life taught me, brought me eventually to a total transformation. I have found new meaning beyond what I even hoped for as a younger man. I would wish the same for you because it has led me to a kind of joy that has been a reward far better than the material and financial success, I started out to achieve.

I say I *would* wish as much for you in recognition of the fact that it may not be the direction you choose to take. You quest may not be for the same kind of fulfillment I have found. That almost goes without saying, because everyone has their own ideas of what success would mean for them., and our definitions of success, the things we believe will ultimately make us happy, are as unique as we are as individuals. Yet, the steps we can take to make our dreams manifest are, at heart, the same.

Unless you were born with a silver spoon in your mouth (forgive me the occasional old saw; I am old, too), having some measure of financial security is a necessary, if not sufficient condition to making even larger goals and manifesting even bigger dreams. Having a foundation of financial security means that you can take certain risks, give things a chance to grow, as well as being better positioned to jump on opportunities whenever and wherever they present themselves. It can mean being able to take a family trip and build the kind of memories that will last a lifetime and beyond. Or, maybe it is having the chance to study, to learn about or how to do something new.

Maybe you have a brilliant idea that most people think is a crackpot notion or a pipedream. So many truly innovative ideas and inventions have languished for lack of the backing, only to arise in a somewhat different form years later. Being able to provide the seed money for yourself is a worthy goal, and it may be that something you learn here about how I made my fortune in real estate will trigger you to try it as stepping stone to what you really want to accomplish in the world.

Don't get me wrong, there is a solid helping of good, practical advice on building a real estate empire of your very own. What's more, I don't stop there. The fact is, by picking up and reading this book, you are doing me a favor. And I don't like to let favors go unappreciated. Reach out to me, if you have the urge, and the wherewithal to *really* follow through, the guts and gumption (I told you, I'm old) to persist and apply the effort, I stand ready to help, directly. Just ask. In the final analysis, though, what you are holding in your hands is an invitation to change – to transform.

Transformation can be difficult at times. It takes dedication, constant effort and that inestimable quality called grit to keep moving forward, and to achieve never-ending progress and improvement as you go. If it were easy, everybody would be doing it, all the time. We all know directed, focused, change is hard – anyone who's ever gone on a diet or started an exercise regimen, or set themselves to learning a foreign language, or any new skill, have found that this takes time and effort, and the willingness to not do so well and learn from your mistakes. And, as we've all found out, making the commitment is easier than keeping it.

This it is also necessary work, and I am dedicated to making it easier for you to succeed, by sharing the formulas that have worked for me. If your old ways of thinking and doing were getting you everything you wanted of them, you would not be reading this sentence.

This book serves as my promise to you that transformation is possible for every one of you as surely as it has been for me. I know that in my life it has proved to be a reward worth every ounce of effort that it required to find my way to it.

I feel I can promise as much for you because the whole process I have followed myself, and laid out here for you, from freeing your imagination to dream bigger, to setting out the practical steps to making them reality, have worked time after time, for me and for others I have mentored, taught, learned from, and followed. Finding the will power and dedication to keep applying yourself, driving yourself toward your dream, and building it up piece by piece, is the final determinant of how far you can go.

Having created the life of my dreams, I am now committed to helping you to do the same. The place to begin your transformation is learning to think like an investor. That, then, is where this book begins.

PART 1 - THINK LIKE AN INVESTOR

DESIRE

"The starting point of all achievement is desire." – Napoleon Hill

All great successes in life come from our thoughts. Before we achieve, we must first conceive. But our thoughts must be infused with a burning desire.

Having that burning desire is essential to continued movement in the direction of what we wane.

I have found this to be true in anything I have wanted to accomplish. Along the journey of greatness there will always be obstacles and challenges. To push through them, you must cultivate a burning desire and let nothing get in its way. It's your rocket fuel.

Any achiever understands that a burning desire comes before any great achievement. You have to want it so bad you can taste it.

A burning desire creates a state of mind that will generate the energy and vibrations to attract all that you need to accomplish what you want. A burning desire drives action.

A burning desire permeates and penetrates every cell of your being. It clarifies your thinking and motivates exactly what you need to do to achieve your goals.

This is not to say other parts of your life are unimportant. But to achieve e your dreams, you must have a set of priorities that direct each day's activities. Making progress toward life goals will energize every part of your life.

When you have a burning desire and can work your mind and energy into a goal-oriented frenzy, you'll begin to notice how life will fall into place. Fortunate "coincidences" will begin to unfold as you apply the universal laws of energy.

When I was a young man, just over 21, I made the decision to begin my real estate career I remember how passionate I was and my willingness to do anything I could to have the freedom I envisioned as my future. I read books, watched infomercials, studied people who had what I wanted to attain, and made a decision to do whatever it takes. I had a burning desire.

What I didn't have was money. I actually called my parents to see if they'd help me buy that first house, and they said no. Being a defiant child, this made me all the more determined! Another path opened up before me. It wasn't long before I had my first success.

It was a burning desire that got me chat first house. Without a burning desire, I might have accepted that "no" and settled for less in life.

I took my desire and ran with it, and before I was 25 years old, I had accumulated over 100 rental properties in Phoenix, Arizona.

I wish I could say that it just got better from there. But life wasn't done teaching me. (It never really is, if you pay attention.) There were lessons needed to learn to get to where I am today.

At 41 years old, I had to start all over again, and a burning desire isn't just for the young! I was able to tap back into the creative force, get that burning desire fired up again. This time I had more than just a burning desire. I took what I'd learned from success and from disaster and implemented the strategies that I will share in the remaining chapters in this book.

DECISION

"Nothing happens until you decide. Make a decision and watch your life move forward" – Oprah Winfrey

Making a decision is a powerful act. It directs your burning desire toward a plan of action.

I sit here in Breckenridge writing this book that I've wanted to write for at least two decades, and since you're reading it, it's now a reality. My burning desire to write it was finally strong enough to overcome that inertia. So, I made a decision it would be finished by the end of January. I made a plan of action, and the universe - the energy web, if you will - has led me to the right places and the right people at the right moments.

Without a derision, your burning desire is useless. Many people desire to do many things

- quit smoking, lose weight, master a new skill - but fail to make the firm, unshakeable decision that makes it happen.

A committed decision is the key to defined purposeful action.

If your burning desire and commitment is to make real estate your path to financial freedom, you must determine what area of real estate you want to pursue. There are incredible opportunities in this field, but only deciding which area you want to specialize in can help you determine exactly what action to take whatever you may choose, a burning desire and a committed decision are your fuel and your North Star.

At 41 years old, basically broke, I found my burning desire still alight inside me. I made a committed decision to get back into real estate and set a goal of having 50 rentals by the time I was 50. I wrote it on a

3 x 5 card and imprinted that image on my brain every day. I visualized what it would mean to me, felt the feelings that would come with success.

Think It. Feel It. Achieve It

By the time I was 49, I had reached my goal of 50 rentals and I was living the life of my dreams.

When you reach a certain goal your view changes. Do the process again: find your next burning desire, commit to your next goal, and let your decision guide your choices in every way.

The mind can only achieve what the mind can see.

Most successful people make decisions quickly and change their minds slowly once a decision has been reached. People who make decisions quickly and firmly, who have a burning desire and definiteness of purpose, generally get what they want.

Once you have decided to move forward, in your real estate career or in any endeavor that matters to you, it is imperative to get into action immediately. Start to learn everything you can about your geographical area, the market, and the area of real estate you want to pursue. If you find a mentor who has what you want, make an alliance, and learn from someone who has been there and done that. Genuinely successful people are often happy to share what they know.

You'll want to find the reason why you want to be in real estate and understand what it will do for you. (I am using real estate as an example because it is what I know, but the method of a burning desire plus committed decision plus purposeful action works for any goal.)

The bigger your why, the more you will stay committed co following your dreams. It's your why that drives your desire, so there is no such thing as understanding it too thoroughly.

"What the mind can conceive and believe. and the heart desires. you can achieve." Norman Vincent Peale

THOUGHTS

"Creativity is intelligence having fun" - *Albert Einstein*
"Change your thoughts and you change your world."
- Norman Vincent Peale

We have all heard the time-honored saying that thoughts are things. "As a man thinketh, so is he." This truth is the reason we need co train ourselves to think in a certain way. Our repeated thoughts shape our lives. Everything we see, do, or have, whether we find it pleasant or not, has been created by our thinking.

T-W-A-H-C-D

Thoughts-Words-Actions-Habits-Choices-Destiny

Our thoughts are the words we say co ourselves, and this self-talk ls the most important conversation you'll ever have. You must direct your thinking in ways that support getting everything you want.

Sound easy? Changing a habit of mind is never easy. Once you fully understand this, you will find it an enormous challenge. Most of us are conditioned to negative and ineffective thinking. But you must persevere because aligning your self- talk with a burning desire and committed decision is the most important thing you can do.

The words we tell ourselves will direct the actions that we take. Listen to your inner voice. Is it positive? Determined? Enthusiastic?

Are you replaying old mental "tapes" of self- doubt, fear or resentment? It takes time, but you can replace those with positive messages and goal-oriented thinking.

Thoughts lead to actions. Actions, repeated daily, become the habits that make us who we are.

Learn to direct your thinking and your actions will fall into place and become positive habits.

The habits we practice create our character and ultimately the destiny that awaits us. We are what we do.

The good news: The choice is yours! When we understand that it is our thinking that determines our direction in our life, we begin to understand the importance of disciplined, conscious thinking. You can direct your mind to direct your energy, and you will find that when your thoughts are aligned with a burning desire and decision, you1re tapping into the energy and wisdom of the universe.

All day long, starting when you awaken, consciously cultivate the feelings and thoughts you want in your world. Your mind is your private place of power; what you think about creates your reality. If negative thoughts arise, don't beat yourself up. Observe them with detachment. They're just the echo of old habits. Let them fade, refocus, and carry 0n visualizing and strategizing toward your goal.

Cultivate a thought process that will move you in the direction of what you want to achieve.

Once you begin taking charge of your life by directing your thoughts, you will want be sure your priorities are in order. What is important to you? The clearer your priorities, the greater your ability to direct all your thoughts to building the life of your dreams.

Remember, this is your life, it is important. You matter! Make your burning desire, your decision, and your goals a priority. The people who truly love you will be cheering you on.

THE IMPORTANCE OF GRATITUDE

You're rewiring your mind, creating new neural pathways. One of the best starting points is gratitude. Just about all of us have moments of gratitude in any given day, but to focus your thoughts on gratitude on a daily basis takes some practice.

Start each day by listing the things you're grateful for. Take a little time to visualize and cherish each one in detail. Make space for a simple gratitude practice as part of your morning routine, even if it means getting up a few minutes early,

The wonderful thing about a gratitude practice is that you'll see immediate effects on your mood, and that's a powerful motivator and energizer.

With a grateful heart, set your intention for the day. Say it aloud to yourself. Write it down. (A gratitude and intention journal can be a wonderful aid.) "Today I will __ because ____."

Taste your burning desire to make it happen.

Getting my mind in a good place and focusing on what I want to accomplish for the day has always worked for me. Remember, we get to choose what we think, which will determine how we feel and what we do. Gratitude and clear intention feels good. Feeling good and having a good vibration field will draw still more good into your life.

Everything is energy. Physicists have proven this scientific fact. There is an energy web that runs through everything, and the higher the frequency we put out, the better our life will unfold. Make it your first job every day to get yourself vibrating at a high frequency.

Thoughts are things. That is why the way we think is so important. The things we read or watch, the people we associate with, all affect the energy we put into the world. Build your thoughts with care, nourish them with quality input from mentors and other worthwhile sources.

Your life experience is a direct expression of your inner thoughts.

Directing your thinking is the most important process in creating your life exactly as you want it.

"Your world is your kaleidoscope; you choose the colors you see"·- Marc Pelletz

FAITH

"We never grow closer to God when we just live life. It takes deliberate. pursuit and attentiveness." - Francis Chan

There are two kinds of people in the world, those who think they can, and those who think they can't. They are both correct according to their faith.

Faith is something that can be created by experience, repetition and practice. Just like going to the gym on a regular basis or practicing anything you want to get good at, it takes time and commitment.

Faith activated sets energy in motion to allow everything in your heart's desires to manifest.

There is no better feeling than the heartfelt faith that God, source, spirit, energy or whatever you wish to call it is working and conspiring with you to create the life of your dreams.

Looking back at the last 20-plus years of my life, I've made it a habit of connecting with my higher power. I call It God. It doesn't matter what you call it or what your religious beliefs are; what is important is connecting with the Universal Creative Source. Artists, musicians and scientist rely on it all the time; it's here for real estate investors and everyone else too.

The more time you spend connecting with the Source, the more you will trust It and your faith will grow.

You are co-creating your life experience with this intelligent energy. Adding your increasing, reality-based faith to your burning desire and committed decision makes anything and everything possible. You will find that you truly can achieve whatever you can conceive.

God, the Universal Source, is part of us and we are part of It, whether you're most comfortable with a personal God, an understanding of quantum physics, or some other modality. Our desire, thoughts and commitment are the way we communicate with this all knowing being that is what we are made of.

We are made in the image and likeness of God, and when we truly believe this, we will know without a shadow of a doubt that all things are possible. There are many different pathways to connect with Universal Energy.

Over 20 years ago, I began a practice of writing to God (who I freely admit, I didn't know or understand) each morning when I woke up. Along with a gratitude practice, it became a part of my daily routine, and I soon saw the results. Thus, began my certainty that there is a power that will guide and help me in all of life's journey.

The more time I spend communicating with God each day, the closer I get to the Source and the greater my faith is. Today, I understand "Ask and you shall receive," not as a pleasant saying, but as my objective reality. And the closer you get to the Source, the more peace, contentment and trust you will have.

Make this energy your friend and you will learn how to transform your desires into your reality.

I will ask you to keep an open mind and reach out. It doesn't matter what your past beliefs or upbringing are. There is a power available to us all, but it takes a desire to find it and build a relationship with it.

A morning ritual that gets your day started with gratitude and intentions expressed directly to this power will go a long way to create the life of your dreams.

In the morning we can create a reality-based positive mindset for ourselves beginning with a clear picture of what we are grateful for, what we desire and what we wish to become, imprinting new beliefs through habits that support our vision.

Everything exists for us as a possibility once we have built an unshakable faith.

We must understand the incredible power of repetition and habit. Don't be fooled into thinking there is any other way to change your subconscious.

All of the suggestions in this booklet need to be practiced and repeated daily to affect your neural pathways and bring about the reality of your dreams.

There is a thinking stuff from which all things are made that permeates and penetrates and fills the interspaces of the universe.

A thought in this substance will produce the image held in that thought.

Gratitude unifies your mind with that source, so your thoughts are received by that of which all is formed.

The vision of what is possible takes hold, and our realities and priorities change accordingly.

"Set your life on fire." – Rumi

GOALS

"Do what you can with what you have, where you are."
-Theodore Roosevelt

I am sure you have heard this before, but have you actually done it? Have you really written down your goals and shared them with someone else?

If you have never done this before, this act alone will be a starting point in taking the action towards anything you want in life.

If you don't have goals, you don't have a target to hit. How will you know that you have arrived?

Setting goals is one action that most won't undertake. It sounds too simple or too trite or too difficult. To be successful in life or real estate, you must be willing to do what most will not do.

Be a winner. Set your goals.

The more specific your goals are, the better this works.

The universe or energy web has a way of conspiring to give you all of your heart's desires, but It has to know what they are.

When I began goal setting when I was just over 20 year's old. I began a practice of writing down my goals on index cards that 1 placed in my car, by my bed and on my desk. 1 wanted to continually imprint my mind with all of my specific desires.

This is a good time to get all your priorities in order, nor just your business or real estate goals but all of them. The cleaner and clearer picture you have of what you want your life to look like, the better it will be.

Keep in mind that your goals can have some flexibility. You will only be able to envision what you can see from where you are right now. As your perspective evolves, so will your goals.

When goals are activated by a burning desire, underlined by a committed decision, and informed with daily gratitude practice and an unshakable faith, the thought will be fully impressed on intelligent source and will transmute into reality.

Make sure you have some short- and long-term goals. Make small goals that you can achieve daily, taking action steps in the direction of what you want. You'll start to see your progress.

When I began to acquire properties, I made a goal of looking at a minimum of five houses a day. This was an action I could take every day toward a larger goal: buying one house every week. I knew these actions were practical steps toward my desired destination.

BE AN ACTION TAKER!

To develop a magically potent mindset, begin these daily habits. Build your temple within.

Magically potent beliefs are imprinted into your subconscious according to what you believe is possible.

To build ourselves with purpose and vision based on the model of reality I'm describing here, is the ultimate creative act.

Start today by making goals and moving in the direction of everything you have ever desired.

Remember this is your life. If you want to accomplish more, be more and have more, begin now. Making goals will be your blueprint, guiding your actions and channeling your burning desire.

Activate the intelligence that wants all your desires to be fulfilled. I challenge you, pick up a pen and paper and do it right now. Don't wait. Something wonderful is beginning.

"Enthusiasm is one of the most powerful engines of success.

When you do a thing do it with your whole might. Put your whole soul into it. stamp it with your personality.

Be active. Be energetic. Be enthusiastic and faithful and you will accomplish your object.

Nothing great was ever achieved without enthusiasm."
- Ralph Waldo Emerson

SPECIALIZED KNOWLEDGE

"Specialized knowledge combined with right thoughts will move you in the direction of the images imprinted in your mind." - Marc Pelletz

There are all kinds of knowledge, but only knowledge applied in an organized manner will help you move in the direction of your goals.

In this book, we are talking about educating your mind to move in the direction of your desires. All true learning takes place through experience, so if you wish to be truly educated, don't just read these suggestions. Do them. Once educated that way, you will be able to take these principles and, with continued practice, be able to achieve anything your mind can envision.

In real estate there are so many areas of opportunity and so much to know that you will want to focus, build your expertise and specialize in a particular area. My area of expertise is flipping houses, rental and rehabbing in a specific geographic area.

When I started my investing career, I read all the books and listened to all the tapes I could find on the philosophy I'm describing. I also trained myself to think like all expert, studying different ways to invest with creative financing. At the time I didn't have money, so creative financing was definitely called for.

Once I begin taking action on the desires I had, the universe began conspiring to give me everything I needed.

You don't have to be the expert on everything. Forming a mastermind group with others who have complementary skills will add to the energy field you're building, an energy field that will magnify and attract all that is needed.

Get involved in real estate clubs and networking organizations in the area you're working. It will help you to build your team.

When I began my career in real estate the second time, in Florida. I knew that I must understand value, so I began that habit of looking at 5 to 10 houses each day. Soon I had mastered the art and science of property evaluation and knew exactly how to size up a prospective investment giving me the ability to act quickly and decisively.

All skills, in real estate and any other field can be learned. When we have a burning desire and cultivate the discipline of great habits - gratitude, intention setting, faith, and clear clean priorities and goals- all things are possible.

In my real estate career, I have rehabbed and sold over 1000 properties, and in the last 10 years I've done over $100 million in rehabbed flips. I did all of this without knowing anything about construction. Zip. I don't have to.

Early in my career, I began building my network at real estate investment meetings and clubs. The contractor I met 20 years ago via my network is still with me today. The universal energy field connected us.

Align your energy with the source by cultivating these habits. Take action toward what you want. The universe will continue to provide all that is needed. It works for me; it will work for you.

You do need to actually adopt the habits, take constructive actions, and rewire your neural pathways for abundance and success. You can't just read about it and think, "I should do that sometime" handy as that might be, it doesn't work that way.

But you'll find yourself enjoying the process. It's a refreshing way to live.

Please be patient. Sometimes things manifest quickly and sometimes slowly, but they will always manifest if we have a burning desire, maintain our gratitude, set out intentions and carry out actions that bring us closer to our goals. Don't quit. Have fun.

What you become on this journey of mind training and motivational muscle building, in real estate or any other field, will determine the level of success you will achieve. The knowledge you gather in your specialized field is important, but secondary.

The primary skill that will move you toward your dream of financial freedom and independence will be establishing these habits of mind and action. Count your gratitude. See your intention. Commune with your higher power about it all. Write down your goals and keep them always in your field of vision.

Whenever you go, there you are." Take consistent, continued daily action. Build these habits. Train your mind to think in ways that energize you and support your success.

To achieve success in any area, our beliefs must serve us. As we sow, we will reap; it's a universal law, and we must begin to think in a certain way to be on the right side of it. Once

you have begun rewiring your habits and training your mind, you will find that it's becoming your nature. All things considered; it is a lot less difficult than continuing to sabotage yourself with negative assumptions.

Once we make a dear decision and implement these practices, we change the vibration of energy we are sending into the universal energy web. (Once again, everything is energy. We are energy. Money is energy. Communication is energy. Properties are energy.)

It's our daily duty to our true selves and each other: to raise our vibrations through our thoughts and actions, so that we will attract abundance and success in our lives. As we send out higher vibrations, the energy web sends back higher results.

As our beliefs continue to shape out reality our new found reality continues to refine our beliefs. Fresh sources of gratitude multiply. intentions clarify. Creativity flourishes. It becomes our priority to imprint positive images and beliefs on a daily basis, to continue to rewire our neural pathways.

The knowledge contained in this book is but a beginning. Where you are today is the cumulative result of all your thoughts, habits and actions so far. What you attract, you become.

Your innermost thoughts and desires ate what shape your character and destiny, and all of it is within your control with a properly trained mind.

Become all you can be. Good thoughts backed by continued right actions will always produce like results, just as bad thoughts can never produce good results. Like produces like. You cannot choose your starting point, but I promise you, you can choose your next moves. By imprinting your thoughts on a burning desire, you can definitely shape your circumstances moving forward.

Remember, successful people are willing to do what unsuccessful people are not.

Technical knowledge in your area of real estate or life will be important to your success, but it will be secondary to your thinking process.

One thought, one decision, one day at a time, take baby steps in the direction of fulfilling your burning desire.

Make the first decision today. "I will become all that I can become by training my thought process."

To build our model of reality consciously, with purpose and vision, is the ultimate creative act.

BUILDING YOUR TEAM

"Coming together is a beginning. Keeping together is progress. Working together is success." - Henry ford

This chapter will examine team building in a real estate investing context. There are principals here that can apply to any independent business venture, whether it's real estate or catering or massage therapy.

Once you have decided to make real estate investing your career, it is important to build a team.

At first, you need to surround yourself with a small group or professionals. Include a good attorney who specializes in real estate and an accountant. It's important to set up your company and do things the right way from the start. Having the right structure and accounting practices will help you to avoid issues that could cost you money in the future.

As you begin to invest, you will want to build your team further. Whether it is people who will handle marketing, management, or construction, you will want to build relationships in a certain way·

Set a tone from the beginning. Consider these people your partners on the road to your dreams. Get to know them as people. Build you inner circle with trust, honesty, and communication. Seek to inspire. As the saying goes, they don't care how much you know till they know how much you care.

It may be tempting to find the least expensive people to do the jobs, but this is not always the best way. As they say, you usually get what you pay for.

Always do what you say you'll do. Pay when payment is due. Be a person of integrity in all situations. Nothing will take you further than always being responsible and doing the right thing. It's another way of keeping the vibrations on the highest level and recruiting the universe to your cause.

Find the right people and delegate. If you are going to build a rental portfolio, it's best to hire a property manager to handle your rentals sooner rather than later.

You may think doing your own property management will save money or give you tighter control. But a good property management company will save your time, money and aggravation. If you really want to have a life and financial freedom, it's wise to start doing things in a certain way from the start.

It took me a little time before I was able to let go of managing my own properties. But once I did, I was able to scale my business, take vacations and actually make more money.

Each of us has different abilities. Make an honest self-assessment and decide what your interests, strengths and weakness are, then begin to piece together the team to complement your abilities and fill in the gaps.

As your business continues to grow, you will want to surround yourself with key people that understand your long- and short-term goals. Getting your people involved, making them feel special, and letting them know you care goes a long way in building a team that will be beside you for the duration.

Share your mindset freely. Helping other people get what they desire goes a long way toward keeping a group together for a long time, and helps you to achieve your goals. Avoid "'preaching," but demonstrate by your example the benefits of a burning desire, gratitude, focused intention, goal setting and action. Create a positive feedback loop: you, your team, and the universal creative force.

Keep in mind, you are in this for the duration. You have a burning desire to succeed in real estate and build the life of your dreams. So, take no shortcuts in choosing and nurturing the team. Decide what type of company you want to create and begin to assemble the team with clear, defined intention, and you'll create a future that you can be proud of.

We can accomplish more as a team than we can ever do by ourselves.

It is the journey that really matters. Build your team wisely, with intention, and you will have taken major strides in the direction of a future beyond your wildest dreams.

GRATITUDE

"Cultivate the habit of gratitude for every good thing that comes to you and give thanks continuously. And because all things have contributed to your advancement, you should include all things in your advancement." - Ralph Waldo Emerson

Gratitude is the elixir that activates a closer connection to intelligent substance.

When we have a graceful attitude, all the little things in life that can get in the way of our joy and happiness disappear.

An attitude of gratitude needs to be cultivated and practiced. A daily routine is best.

Start and end each day by thinking of three things you are grateful for. Spend at least one minute on each of them. Implant the feelings of gratitude into your whole being. Doing this practice morning and night will speed and reinforce the process of changing your neural pathways.

Being in and thinking from a place of gratitude bring us into harmony with all that is available.

When we live life with a feeling of gratitude, our energy vibrates at a higher frequency. Make it a daily goal to vibrate at the highest frequency possible.

Remember, this does take practice. To create change, we must make it a habit to be grateful.

You have heard it before: attitude creates altitude. Life is defined not by what happens to us, which we cannot control, but by our attitude to and perception of what happens.

I used to think I had lots of problems. Usually, I would blame someone else for them. As I began to grow, and learn, problems became challenges, which was a better way to look at things. As I cultivate a grateful attitude, all of my challenges became opportunities to learn and grow.

Learning and growing is a good thing. Reframing problems as learning opportunities is a much more useful way to perceive things.

When we believe like this, we are liberated.

Everything that happens to us is good.

There's an ancient Latin saying: Amor fati. Love your fate. When you can embrace all that happens as it just is, with acceptance and a peaceful mind, the practice of gratitude has been finally imprinted on your own subconscious.

The grateful mind continues to expect good things to happen, and this creates more good in your life. A feeling of "everything I touch turns to gold" is an energy that actively creates reality, just like someone who constantly says "Nothing ever works out for me, I only have awful luck," is likely to keep experiencing exactly that reality.

This gets us back to our original premise. Thoughts are things, and when we accept this as the truth, we realize the importance of directing our own thinking.

Thought impressed on intelligent substance will transmute and become that which we think about.

Therefore, it is of utmost importance to start the practice of gratitude.

When we have implemented the practice of gratitude so consistently that it is our natural state, and we embrace challenge with exuberance, anything and everything that happens is transformed.

Minor nuisances of life will be learning opportunities instead of problems, and still more opportunities will appear on your horizons. Your body and mind will begin to function like a GPS. Anytime you make a wrong turn or think a thought that doesn't serve you, you'll find that you can automatically reset and get to gratitude.

When your thinking is directed by your consciousness in a way that serves you and is connected to intelligent source, your decision making operates at a high level. Make it a practice to raise your vibration by activating the power of gratitude daily·

Each of us has the responsibility to choose visions and attitudes that will empower us. It's free. It's something any human being can choose to do.

So choose today to start the practice of gratitude, and watch as your life unfolds in a magical way.

INVESTMENTS: STAND ALONE PROPERTIES

"When you buy stand-alone properties, it is only matter of time before you experience financial freedom." - Marc Pelletz

Each time I began in real estate, I didn't have money. I had to make sure that every property that I bought could "stand alone". What that means is that when I buy a property, it needs to rent for enough money to cover all the expenses: taxes, insurance, vacancies, repairs and management. When I began my career, I knew I wanted a portfolio of stand-alone rentals and would do whatever necessary to acquire them.

It was important that each property have positive cash flow. That is why I started with multi-family properties, which seem to work better as stand alone. My goal was to acquire as many as possible, collect rents, and pay down the mortgage balances. I practiced constant, consistent daily action toward that goal. If you intend to be in real estate for the long haul, this is the best way to build financial freedom.

Wherever you are in your real estate career, I think you will agree that $10,000 per month in positive cash flow makes a good first goal to strive for. Start with a plan. Train your mind. Be patient. Constant movement in the direction of what you want will give you rewards.

Do not get distracted by thinking this is the wrong time to buy. There are always opportunities in all real estate cycles. It is always time to buy if you can structure the deal to meet your needs and buy stand-alone properties.

When I bought my first small apartment complex, I didn't know it at the time, but it turned out I'd bought at the highest point of the market. My asset sheet fluctuated in value, but the cash flow basically stayed the same. At one point, the value dropped to $500,000; at another it was $1.5 million. But I bought this property for my future, and the cash flow from it never changed. Almost 20 years later, it has paid itself off, and I simply get a rent check every month.

That's what building a rental portfolio of stand-alone properties and consistently paying down mortgages will do: lead you to freedom. If you'd like a life of freedom, real estate rental properties are the best way to go, especially when you have the right management to handle them. Whether your goal is 10 houses, 100 properties or 1000 rentals, you can begin your process now.

GIVING BACK

"Only by giving you are able to receive more than you already have." - Jim Rohn

The more we give, the more we get. I have found this to be true throughout my life.

As Zig Ziglar says, "You can get everything in life you want if you will just help enough other people get what they want."

One of the greatest gifts of being a successful real estate investor is having the financial freedom and time to be more, to have more and to do more.

We continue to grow as individuals as we move from survival mode to success to having ever greater ability to make a difference and contribute in the world.

We continue to grow, cultivating thoughts and practices that move us in the direction of all of our dreams and desires.

As we evolve into fully integrated individuals, we find that place in our hearts that desires to give back and make a difference growing stronger and clearer each day. Gratitude inspires us. A burning desire drives us.

Right now, today, no matter where you are, there is some small thing you can do that will make another person's day better. Something you can give. Find it. Do it. Be grateful for it. Do another one tomorrow.

Now imagine having the time and financial resources to find ways to make lots of things better for lots of people. Take it from me. It's a lot of fun.

"We make a living by what we do, but we make a life by what we give."
- Winston Churchill

HABITS - PUTTING IT ALL TOGETHER

"Good habits are crafted in the workshop of everyday life." - Marc Pelletz

We understand now that thoughts are things, and that we have the ability to direct our thinking to create the life of our dreams.

To do this and to actively change our neural pathways we know that we must implement new habits and keep practicing them diligently until the neural pathways are rewired and the reward cycle kicks in, by which time you will be hooked.

Our thoughts direct the words we say to ourselves and others. These words direct our actions and habits, which in turn create our character and destiny. The road to fulfillment, the road to success, and the high road are one and the same path.

It is our responsibility on a daily basis to implement disciplines which will move us in the direction of our desires. When we do that, we stop blaming other people or bad luck or anything else and develop the ability to manifest what we need.

As I sit here finishing this booklet that I have had a desire to write for more than 3 decades, it is apparent to me that I followed the formula outlined in this book to make it happen.

About 3 months ago, I made a decision: that when I came to Breckenridge for Christmas and New Years, I would write this book. I have had a desire to do it for years. I worked myself into a burning desire, set a deadline, and shared with several of my partners. We made a date for a seminar to coincide with the launch of this book, Think Like a Real Estate Investor. The intention was firmly established.

I set my goal. Each day I would complete one chapter.

Now watch what the universe did. What God's brought to the table.

Before I came here I met a guy, Eric, while I was doing a real estate deal. He connected me with his friend Pete, who lives here in Breckenridge. It turns out Pete has written several books. We connected, and with his help and resources, my plan to have this book completed has been expedited. I'm ahead of schedule, and the pieces just keep falling into place.

There you go. That's manifestation. You're reading it right now. That's what happens when we direct our thinking, fueled by a burning desire.

Daily persistent action in the direction of what I want has led to this book being written in less than two weeks.

This book is meant to be a starting point for your success in real estate investing. The mind training principles and habits are useful to anyone desiring to walk a prosperous and honorable path.

Each chapter gives you a nugget of insight into necessary steps, a template on which to build each day.

You will want to continue to learn all about the area of real estate you choose, while understanding that it is your thoughts that create your reality.

Spend time daily directing your thinking. Build an unwavering belief that you will create everything your heart desires.

Take this information and run with it. Implement a daily practice of directing your thoughts. Practice gratitude. You will build a life that you are consciously co-creating each day with the Universal Source as a partner on your team.

How far and fast you travel will be dependent on your commitment to excellence and your daily practice of directing your thinking, backed by faith.

SUMMARY

Hopefully, you have found some wisdom in this blend of mind training strategies and beginning real estate tips that will motivate and inspire you to start today.

Implement these techniques on a daily basis, and begin to watch as the magic unfolds and things fall into place as thoughts aline with the creative source. Thoughts are things, and it is our responsibility to shape our thoughts and direct our thinking in ways that move us in the direction of our heart's desires.

Each of these chapters is but a starting point. Every action described in this book will take a commitment to daily practice and consistent improvement.

In creating the life of our dreams, what we do for a living is not as important as what we become.

Real estate can be the vehicle that allows us to grow: to become more, to have more and to help others.

I hope you find this book helpful and that it leads you on your journey to joy, fulfillment and financial freedom.

SUGGESTED READINGS

1. Think and Grow Rich *Napoleon Hill*
2. The Science of Getting Rich *Wallace Wattles*
3. Philosophy of Successful Living *Jim Rohn*
4. The Magic of Thinking Big *David Swartz*
5. The Bible

6. There's a Spiritual Solution to Every Problem *Wayne Dyer*
7. The Success Principles *Jack Canfield*
8. Unlimited Power *Tony Robbins*
9. Quantum Warrior *John Kehoe*
10. Science of Mind *Ernest Holmes*
11. Awaken the Giant Within *Tony Robbins*
12. Power of Intention *Wayne Dyer*

For more information please contact

Marc Pelletz

15 Paradise Place #164

Sarasota, FL 34239

mspelletz@aol.com

Any and all feedback is appreciated.

If you made it this far send an email to mspelletz@aol.com for 25% off my next book or event.

PART 2 – TIME TO MASTER THE GAME OF LIFE

NOT AGAIN (OR, WHY ME?)

Picking this book up off the shelf, or even before deciding to pick it up, the question went through your head, *"What, another book on how to make a fortune in real estate? Why?"*

And I have to admit, it's a fair question. In fact, it's one I needed to answer for myself before I committed my time and energy to writing it. Because, now in my seventies, my energy, and especially the time I have left to me are valuable.

The answer is, this isn't really a book about being successful in real estate, although, as you read it, you will learn a great deal about how to succeed in the real estate business and what kinds of opportunities there are to make yourself as rich as you imagine. I'm passionate about people, maybe even more than I am passionate about financial freedom. I'm not doing this at all for money.

I will tell you how I did it, starting with nothing, twice. And I will tell you some of the paths I did not pursue in building my real estate businesses that might be better suited to your own situation and inclinations.

I'm interested in making a difference in the world by helping you learn to reshape your behaviors by opening your mind to new possibilities. Real estate is one example, but more than that, it is a core way to fund things right now. I'm not even all that interested in real estate right now personally, except for the money that it generates for me to do what I want to do. I'm past my sixth decade already and I have made my fortune, a few times, in fact. So, I have reached another stage.

My new goal is to help lift other people up, just as I have been elevated. That can mean many things. To be sure, the broadest reach I can have is with this book – it can be shared with the widest possible audience, and kept around for future reference. There are also my seminars, reaching far fewer people at one time, but with more immediacy and the intensity of being together. There are even mentoring possibilities or more that I might be able to do on a one-to-one basis.

In any case, I am going to take you, step-by-step through not only the process that I used to find success through real estate but a number of avenues to equal or greater success that others have taken instead of mine.

People who read this book want freedom. You may think you are going to find freedom through real estate. Certainly, financial freedom was one of the main things I wanted when I started out in the business, and I certainly have attained it. But the truth is, my freedom didn't come from real estate. It came from the desire and determination, and the courage to go out and try.

We're all looking for fulfillment in our life. There's a science to getting rich. There's is a science in doing real estate, there's a science of getting in shape. But there's no exact science to being fulfilled. But if you're not enjoying what you're doing, you're probably not feeling fulfilled in your life. I can't teach fulfillment because the order fulfillment would be individualized. I can teach you the science of getting rich.

I can teach you how to get in shape. I can teach you how to build a business. I can teach you how to find the girl. Maybe not that one. Maybe I can teach you to keep one. However, wealth is not the same this as fulfillment and getting rich is not always the same as success. That is the real lesson that I've learned. But the path to success and fulfillment are the same steps you take to become a wealthy and successful businessperson in whatever field you choose.

Life is too short to be stuck in doing something you hate. So, having something you're doing that makes you excited and makes you want to wake up in the morning and energizes you and makes you happy and proud of yourself is the important thing.

If you're not doing what you love, you ought to change what you're doing no matter what. Because if you don't find happiness and joy in the vehicle that you're earning money from you, you're probably not going to do a very good job at it. After all, your occupation is what takes up most of your waking hours. If you're not happy doing what you're doing, do what you got to do to change it. don't feel stuck or feel stuck, but do something about it. Because if you're not happy where you working, it's just a JOB. If you're not thinking the right way and you're not happy, you're really not going to create the life that you deserve. Remember what Confucius (yes, the real one) said: "Find a job that you love and never work another day in your life."

No one succeeds entirely on their own, you have to learn how to build a team around you and how to build an inner team within yourself; to make yourself a better human being, so you can attract the right people and build a team to handle the vehicle you want to drive to achieve freedom. Once you have that and you're moving in that direction, you can grow an empire from the inside, out, improved clarity, leveraged to create a better life.

Hopefully, there'll be enough in this book that will open your mind to the possibilities, that you can create the life of your dreams. The information that I'll be giving will hopefully be enough to inspire you to make a change in your life. Decide today is Wake-Up Day. Wake up from the life that I've been living to till today. And decide that tomorrow, I'll take some actions that will make my tomorrows better than they were yesterday.

How I found that path for myself and, hopefully, how I can help you find it with less trial and fewer errors than I had to make (not that mistakes are a bad thing, if you know how to use them – but that's for later) is the reason for this book being in your hands right now. By reading this far, you've already taken the first step.

Bon voyage.

I STARTED WITH NOTHING AND BUILT A FORTUNE, MORE THAN ONCE.

I started out with a normal upbringing in a normal family, decent schools and the opportunity to go to college. I had it better than some, maybe many, but I was no better off and in some cases worse than many others. Add character to the list of my disadvantages – I was a reflexively rebellious child.

I had intelligent parents who encouraged me to read, which I didn't do because I rejected whatever my parents told me. Even so, they were always encouraging, never told me I couldn't do everything; there was nothing that I hadn't done before which I couldn't do.

I started immersing myself in things. I was either in sports or collecting coins or collecting baseball cards, or girls or making money.

Once I got out of college, I headed out to Arizona. I was fortunate enough to meet a guy named Tommy Hopkins who started Champions Unlimited and wrote the book, "Tom Hopkins Guide to Greatness in Sales." He happened to be in an office building right next to me.

Tom Hopkins showed me that I needed to learn from people that knew more than I do. I was starting in the real estate business and he was talking about things that I wanted to know about. I can remember him telling me to walk outside with the client and bring whatever I was selling to life by saying, "Can you just smell the steaks cooking on the grill out here?" and kind of bringing things to life by using adjectives in making people feel like they were in the place. I think he was just a real estate coach at the time, but what I learned from him was different than what he was offering the general public at that time.

I just got inspired about going into business. I got excited and wanted to do some real estate deals. I think I saw a real estate infomercial late one night and told myself, "If they can do that, I can do this." So, I found my first house, for $13,000, and asked my parents to help me buy it.

They weren't about to help me buy a house. They said I didn't know what I was doing. I had just gotten there, they said. In their estimation, I wasn't ready. Being the defiant child that I was, they told me no. I said go. And I made up my mind I was going to go buy a house.

I started listening, reading and studying about real estate. Then, I got my real estate license. I tried being a real estate agent for a short while. It was really good experience for me and it allowed me to learn about the world of real estate from the inside. But I realized that wasn't what I wanted it to be doing. I also went into wholesaling for a very short period of time. I think my first month I made $75,000 wholesaling. I probably have made $1 million wholesaling altogether, but it's really not my thing. Very quickly, I realized that, as much as I loved the energy, the adrenaline rush of the deal, it was addictive.

At the same time, I began to look at it differently. I was lining up deals and projects for other people to make money on, or they wouldn't be taking them. Why was I leaving so much money on the table for them? I had ways to arrange financing; I could hire crews to repair and upgrade the properties. I could make more money by rehabbing myself.

My big money was made from fixing and flipping, all the while holding a portfolio of rental properties. I want to have, I have a team of people that do wholesaling and I make a little bit of on, but it's not my thing anymore, unless I do find properties that I don't want to fix, or they're in neighborhoods that I don't want to buy into because I don't have the infrastructure there. Those are ones that we wholesale now.

The thing is, I made a determination early on that I just wanted to be an investor. So, if I ever got a commission back then, I put it right into investment property. I knew I wanted cash flow. I started by buying rental properties.

I started with small income-producing properties, duplexes and quadplexes, six-plexes and ten-plexes, and single-family homes. For some people, the next step up would be into an apartment complex, mobile home parks, motels, hotels – a whole different arena that has more zeros on it. But the philosophy is always the same. Create cash flow to create a lifestyle to have freedom.

At the beginning of the Internet explosion when advertising and marketing on the Internet were just starting, I was a really good advertising salesman. If I had gotten into what happened on the Internet, I would have been a gazillionaire by tapping into the leverage of what was going on. But it was too intangible. I couldn't see, so I couldn't get a feel for it. I can touch and see and feel real estate, and that solidity made all the difference for me.

Regardless, I made my first millions by the time I was in my mid-twenties.

That wasn't necessarily a good thing. For sure, it was fun, almost as much on the downhill slide as it had been coming up. Before I hit bottom, that is. The way I used to be was, even if I took a wrong position, I would dig my feet in to protect it.

I needed it to be right, just like my father. He had a plaque in his office that read: "I thought that I was wrong once, but I was mistaken," and somebody told me, "The golden rule is: he who makes the gold, makes the rules." I used to live by those two mottos. It was so wrong. It's much better to be wrong and happy than right and miserable.

Back in those days, my morning routine would be a shower, snort a line of cocaine, look for the girl I was with and try to remember where I had gone to bed. Then I'd get dressed and go on my way, and see what would come up next. Cocaine will make you feel like Superman until it turns on you and becomes your kryptonite.

I just kept committing less and less; my standards got lower, my commitment got less. Not so much the commitments I did make to other people. I broke a few but I remained faithful to most of them, even in my worst state of being. But I made fewer of them, and the commitments I had made to myself were the ones I could not, in the end, always keep.

After I became successful, I change the habits that I had. One thing led to the next thing, one bad habit led to another bad habit that got ingrained and became part of who I was. It became part of my conscious and subconscious perception. And a decade later I had gone from successful on the outside to nothing on the outside and the inside.

I can show you how to make several hundreds of thousands of dollars quickly if you learn how to wholesale or flip the right houses and you've got money to play with. But I don't call several hundreds of thousands of dollars rich. I guess if you call it becoming a millionaire in a couple of years quick, I know how to do that, but I don't know how to go from zero to $10 million overnight.

You'll find these young guys that, they do a couple of big deals and the next thing you know, they got a fancy car and a fancy pad and they're flying in a private jet because they just made the money and put it in their pocket and then spending it and the next year that they have nothing that's not rich to me.

To me, rich was always making more than you spend. What these guys do, they make a big paycheck and they spend more than they have. So, before they really have anything, they driving fancy cars and living in fancy places and building a lifestyle that may be sustainable and may not be. Early on when I was young, I suppose I spent in ways different the second time around. So maybe that was a lesson that I learned.

I could have a plane and I could have a fancy house and a fancy car. I even wonder why I don't, but I surely don't want to make that my story because that's not how I live, and I want to attract the type of person who is not necessarily impressed by all of that.

At the same time, I found that I could project an air of confidence by making myself feel rich. So, even when I didn't have much money and I just started to make some, I'd keep $1,000 in my pocket to make me feel rich. When you start to feel a little bit rich, you seem to attract it better. You send out better energy into the world

I made some serious mistakes in my life that I've paid for deeply. One of the big ones is that I didn't get enough trustworthy people involved in places that mattered and my pick for partners was a little bit skewed by the activities that I was engaged in, which were not generally conducive to long-range thinking and good judgment. I was just choosing people that had businesses and fun type energy and probably addicted habits like me that I gravitated toward. I had a long way to fall and it took some time for me to hit bottom. By the time I was forty-one, I was broke again. More, I was mentally, physically, spiritually, emotionally and financially bankrupt.

As soon as my wife got pregnant, I went into rehab because I knew we had problems. My ex-wife couldn't stay sober and I guess neither could I. Not until I left her. I guess I just couldn't stop that insanity that I was caught up in. Getting divorced from my wife and giving up alcohol and drugs, for sure was a huge turning point because success to the outside world began again and the success to the inside world. I started with those habits right then. That's when I began the rituals again, exactly at that critical moment.

Once again, I was determined to make something of myself and my life. I took the idea of Recovery seriously and I began working the twelve steps toward rebuilding my life. I made a connection to my "Higher Power," and admitted, to others first, then eventually to myself, truly, that I did not have the power and self-control to tame my demons on my own. There is always help waiting when you're ready to ask for it.

I started the process of paying attention again to my priorities and what was number one was God, creative intelligence. I started quite simply with, "Good morning, God. Guide me today, lead me to where I'm supposed to go." I had a direction. I had written down on a card what I wanted, and I looked at that and read it all the time and memorized it.

I knew I had done it before, and I had watched other people get successful too. I surely believed that if one person can do it, especially since I had done it before, I could do it again. I knew I could get my life better. I knew if I created systematic rituals and habits that I would get out of where I was, somehow.

Whether you're CEO of a company or looking for your first job, make a decision today that you want to get a little bit better. Like the tortoise in the old story, constant, never-ending improvement moves your life forward in the areas that are important to build a life of happiness and fulfillment. It just takes gradual progress.

I know you're either moving forward or you're moving backward. I had gotten to the place where I was so low there is really only one way to go. And once I started, taking step-by-step actions in the direction of a better life, creating rituals and habits that would make me a better man, things started to come together.

I knew the way out was through real estate because I had done it once before, not that many years prior. I was done with real estate the first time by 1988, until 1998.

I ended up with computer software, a company that automated foreclosures and deed of trust estates that my plan at that time was similar to the plan I have now. It was to go from state to state and get real estate and work with people who are engaged in the business and make connections throughout the country and buy real estate. My philosophy was always just to meet a need to make more money than I was spending.

I make a lot of money now every month, but I don't watch every individual thing that's going on. I'm not a bean counter. Now I've got hundreds of houses. Some of them make me a lot of money, some of them don't, but I'm not paying attention to which ones are and which ones aren't.

The truth of the matter is most businesses fail in some way, shape or form. I had many failed partnerships and I learned from all those failures, lessons that I can apply to the successes that I now have. If it's a learning experience, it's not a failure in the end. I didn't make money on a lot of the things that I got involved in. But I learned some lessons. Being wrong also lets us stay open to other possibilities. Someone just might have something better, or at least that needs to be considered before you close out all possibilities.

People, on average, say no to the things they end up buying five times, even the things they want. Should I buy a new TV today? I want a new TV. Did you see that beautiful new high-definition tv they are selling? I want one. Do you want to go buy it right now? No. On average, they say no five times.

One of the most effective ways to influence people to follow you, whether it's into a real estate deal or a new and uncertain venture, is to speak and act with authority and expertise. What we know about life is knowledge is power, but even more important than that would be self-knowledge is empowerment. Since your unconscious mind is your emotional mind and your conscious mind is your logical mind, all your decisions and choices are made emotionally and rationalized by logic.

People are swayed by authority figures. When you possess the ability to project authority to those around you, others will automatically want to do what you tell them and certainly buy what you are selling – as long as you evidence a total belief in what you are offering.

I started real estate both times with zero money and I did not even know about wholesaling.

I started in creative financing. I created five different kinds of financing structures so I could get involved in real estate with no money, buying property to keep or buying property to flip, or renovate and flip or just to buy it, get possession of it and sell it.

What I found to be true is, when you find a niche and focus on it, you have a very good chance to make yourself financially independent – what many might call rich.

YOUR DESTINATION

I have come to understand, in my late sixties, that the vehicle in which you choose to travel, is much less important than your destination, and how you live your life on the way.

My main credential, as far as others are concerned, is the fact that I've been able to create the financial freedom they seek. Many measure life success in millions of dollars, and fortunately, I've been able to create that kind of wealth.

I know now that what really determined my financial success was less, the actual tools and vehicles I have used, but more, my connection to my God and the way I've learned to live my life.

I am going to share all of that with you, and also I'm going to give you the tools to decide whether the real estate business is right for you, and I'm going to give you a realistic and useful overview to get you started if you choose to follow the path that brought me to financial independence and a life of fulfillment.

THE REAL ESTATE BUSINESS IN A NUTSHELL

It is time to find your niche. Let's start now.

I've promised a roadmap to success, and I intend to keep my word. For the most part, this section will have a lot of practical suggestion on ways to start and grow your real estate business, with different tracks to follow, depending on your goals, your skills and your tolerance for risk

But this is not just a real estate how-to book or one that is only relevant for would-be landlords, house-flippers and the like. The principles that I followed to make my fortunes in real estate are the same ones that will lead to success in any number of endeavors. They are the habits of success and positivity, the harnessing of determination and the willingness to tolerate setbacks but never submit to failure, which only happens when you give up.

WHY REAL ESTATE?

The reason I invested in real estate was because I could see it, I could touch it, I can feel it, and I could collect rent on it. I liked the tangible things that I can actually see. And so, for me, it felt like a less of a mystery than some of those other things that other people invest in. Because my goal was to have income property that would eventually pay for itself, it wouldn't matter what really was happening in the economy or the real estate market, whether the values are rising and falling at any particular time, I can collect my rents from it on a regular basis.

I started small and it wasn't about getting rich quick. It was about a steady growth to having a lifestyle of freedom. Getting rich fast usually doesn't last, and so building something that's sustainable and to give up freedom. My goal was always just to keep making more money than I spent and to keep moving up the ladder that way. I looked at it as something that would provide for me, so I wouldn't have to work someday.

The real estate business is not easy, but it's one of the most lucrative opportunities that anybody can find, whether they start with a little money or a lot, with little knowledge or a lot.

I mention this frequently, and several times in this very book. 90% of millionaires in the U.S. say their primary source of wealth was real estate.

As an aside, the other big builder of wealth in our country is the energy business, which – when you think about it – is also a part of the real estate business.

After all, it was Mark Twain who advised: "Buy land; it's the only thing they're not making more of."

To pick your path in the real estate business or in any other business, think of a matrix, or a chart with two poles- vertical and horizontal. Imagine that the vertical axis is about you, and the horizontal axis is about the industry you are studying. To find your place on the matrix, you must understand both clearly.

IN THE NICHES WE GET RICHES

Choosing your path is about getting to know yourself first and foremost.

So far, we've been talking about the characteristics of the investments themselves. Once you have a basic understanding of the environment, your focus shifts to deciding how all this can fit into the life you are creating for yourself. You get to choose.

What do you love to do, and what do you hate?

Do you love to speculate and to take big chances because you're attracted by the possibility of huge rewards?

Do you love wheeling and dealing, or do you hate? Do you love the challenge of constant negotiation? Does planning your negotiation meeting excite you or make you nervous?

Are you a handy man or woman? Do you love to fix things up and paint them? Do you left to tinker, or do you call a professional at the first sign of an electrical or plumbing problem? Have you enjoyed fixing up your own home, or have you hired people to do every little task?

Moving in the direction of what you love, and away from what you don't love will not only help determine your level of success, but it will be instrumental in determining the quality of your life. If you are smart, your real estate career – or any career, can be a source of joy, fulfillment and satisfaction. Make the wrong decision, and you are in for a life of inconvenience and strife. Clearly, taking your time and getting to know how you fit in could be the most valuable time you ever spend your life.

NICHES

How does real estate build your wealth?

By far, the simplest thing you can do with real estate is own it, provide homes or workplaces for people, and collect rent.

Have you ever wondered, why does real estate make so many people rich? Why is the potential of real estate so great, and why is investing in real estate so powerful?

Because real estate investing has the following wealth-building components that you can't find virtually anywhere else.

CASH FLOW

If you structure it right, your real estate deal will provide monthly cash flow. Let's say your tenant pays you $2000 a month, and your expenses, including taxes and insurance are $1500 a month. Your cash flow is $500. That money comes in no matter whether you work or not, no matter if the news of the day is positive or negative, no matter if the stock market is up or down for the week, month, or year.

Aside from renting to a tenant, another approach is to "sell" the property to a buyer via financing the property yourself, and letting the buyer pay you payments monthly that cover the tenants living, and the purchase of the property. You can also rent the property with an option to buy, which gives a certain amount of time for the buyer to come up with the down payment and qualify for financing. In the meantime you are an income – usually premium income – and the buyer has a home and has locked in a satisfactory purchase price.

CAPITAL GAINS

If you sell a property for more than you paid for it, you are realizing "capital gains." The gain is your profit. If you made the money within a year, you gain is taxed as ordinary income. If you owned the property for more than 12 months before you sold it, you pay less in taxes because you qualify for capital gains tax treatment. The less tax you pay, the more money you make. Smart investors always consider taxes.

BUILDUP OF EQUITY AS YOU PAY OFF YOUR MORTGAGE

The payments on your mortgage include principal and interest. The rent you collect give you the money to make the payments, so the debt is self-liquidating. In a real estate deal, you have someone else paying down your loan and building equity for you. Your tenant goes to work every day, to earn the money to pay a part of his or her paycheck to you month after month and year after year. Imagine five, 10, or 100 people paying you a big part of their paychecks every month for the rest of your life. The more tenants you have, the faster you get wealthy.

BUILDUP OF EQUITY FROM APPRECIATION OF YOUR PROPERTY

Most assets depreciate or go down in value. Real estate, over the long haul, has always gone up in value. There have been cycles, which you must be aware of, but over the long term, property appreciates, and over the long haul, real estate has never failed to keep up or surpass inflation, or the devaluation of money. The most important part of this is the fact that real estate is safe and easy to finance. If you put down $40,000 as down payment on a $200,000 rental property, you are getting the appreciation on the whole $200,000 of value, not just the $40,000 down payment.

TAX SAVINGS

You are allowed to take a tax deduction every year for wear and tear, deterioration, or obsolescence of your property. Generally the leverage is very attractive. First of all you are able to depreciate the entire value of your property over 27.5 years. However, even though, according to your deal with the IRS, your property has lost all of its value, it is probably – in reality – more valuable than it was the day you bought it. When the property is financed the deal is even better. According to the previous example, you are receiving the tax benefits on a $200,000 property, even though you only put $40,000 into it. There is leverage available in other investments, but none as safe and reliable as the leverage you get in a properly selected and designed real estate investment.

How To Start Without Money

WHOLESALING

You have undoubtedly heard somewhere – on infomercials late at night, on websites, in countless books, and in get-rich-quick seminars everywhere, that you can make a lot of money in real estate without having any money of your own. Much of the hype is just that – hype!

When the message is legitimate, they are probably referring to one of the best ways, and one of the only ways to get started making a lot of money in real estate without your own resources - WHOLESALING.

Because this is such a good way to get started, and because all it takes is concentration and work, and is something you can certainly master quickly and easily, I'm going to spend a little bit more time on the details of wholesaling then I will on the other niches.

Again, this book is only meant to give you an overview, and there are many wonderful ways to get enough information to become highly proficient.

I recommend that you study hard and become very proficient at whatever specialty you choose, but to create real success for yourself, you will definitely need more technical information than you are going to get here. Our objective here is to help you choose your path and give you the information you need to get started.

Let's say you are eager to make money in real estate, but don't have the money. Let's say you know that real estate investing can be lucrative, but you also know that it is slow and can be very risky. Let's say you like the idea of lucrative investments, but are reluctant to get involved in being a landlord.

Wholesaling of real estate may very well be exactly what you are looking for.

Wholesaling of real estate means finding a great real estate deal, and then selling it to another party who has the resources, and is interested in buying the deal you found.

You do the difficult work, use your ingenuity to find a great deal, you get that deal under contract, and then you sell that contract to someone else who would like to take over under the terms of your contract.

There are also double closings, and other ways to do this which are beyond the scope of this book, but that information is plainly available, especially from our REI Live organization, where we actually give lessons on wholesaling.

This does not necessarily involve being a realtor, it does not require a license in most states, and you are really not looking to earn income or make money from the property itself. You are operating as a middle-person who sells your position in the contract.

ADVANTAGES OF WHOLESALING REAL ESTATE

First of all, you can have virtually no money of your own in the deal. You may put up earnest money, but there are even clever ways to avoid that. The terms, of course, are completely negotiable between you and the seller, and you can do your part of the deal with as little as a few hundred dollars, or in some cases no money at all!

If you make your deal correctly, you will have virtually no risk of losing your money, even if the deal doesn't work out.

Next, financing is not a concern at all. You don't have to secure financing, which could involve going through lengthy and stressful negotiations, working with lenders, inspections, appraisals or any of those complications.

Because you are not really trying to close the property, and are just aiming to sell the contract to another buyer, you really don't need a loan at all.

Finally, because you never technically take ownership of the property, you never become a landlord, and never have to do repairs or maintenance on the property. You are the owner of a contract, which requires no upkeep, repairs, or carrying costs. This really is as clean as a profitable deal can get.

HERE IS MY STEP-BY-STEP PLAN FOR SUCCESS AS A REAL ESTATE WHOLESALER...

1. Identify a target property. Often, the best candidates are properties that are distressed for some reason. One of my favorite kinds of distressed properties, and one of the most profitable are properties that have been on the market for a long time. As time goes by. Owners become more desperate. They are paying a mortgage on a house they don't live in, or don't want to live in, and you can use their desperation to your advantage. Sites like Cielo and redfin are terrific places to look for these types of deals, and making friends with a real tour, and staying up to date with the multiple listing service can be even better. I said earlier that you don't have to be a licensed realtor, but it certainly doesn't hurt.

   There are other sites, such as Craigslist, and HomesByOwner that make it relatively easy to find deals in your area. Utilize keywords such as MOTIVATED, MUST SELL, AS IS, and FIXER UPPER. You can be even more creative, but these key terms will help you find the deals you are looking for.

2. Do the math. Remember, your objective is to sell a contract, not a property so you must take different costs into account then you would when you are buying a property. Consider title fees, fees you might put out to have a contractor to an evaluation when the house needs repair, using the advice or services of an appraiser. Sometimes, you can get away without paying for the services. People are often eager to help, and you can negotiate the escrow fees and other fees through the title company once you are familiar with the processes.

   If you are going to make a mistake, this may be the place. Make sure you get good numbers to calculate any repairs that might be necessary. You should not avoid properties that need repairs, because those can often be the most profitable, but you must get good numbers and make sure you leave enough room to make a healthy profit, when you make your offer to the owner.

3. Find the owner. You have found the distressed property which is a good candidate, but sometimes you must also do additional work to find the owner, and to find a way to contact them.

   One very inexpensive way to do this is to simply knock on the neighbors' doors and ask if they know the owner. Usually you will find someone who does, and I have found that I can often get the phone number or email address, in order to connect with the owner. There is a service called "skip-tracer" whose job it is to find the name and contact information of the owner. Remember, if you are having a hard time finding the owner, so is everyone else. This may be the opportunity you are looking for, to make a great deal because you have no competition.

4. Negotiate the Contract. Remember, this is no place to be shy. This negotiation is the key to making a great deal. The better deal you are able to make, the easier it will be to find the investor to sell your contract to. You are always eager to make good deals for your buyers, because once you have a stable of buyers, it becomes much easier for you to make your deals, and can become a stable and reliable source of income for you. Ideally, once you get going and achieve some momentum, you know exactly who to call when you find a deal.

   A negotiating hint: don't forget to remind your seller that there are going to be no upfront fees, because there are not going to be any realtors involved in the deal. Remind the seller that closing costs and escrow fees are going to be covered, and that you will handle all the details of the purchase.

For a distressed seller, these can be very valuable triggers that will motivate that seller to drop his price lower than he ever thought he would.

Always make sure you are giving yourself an escape route, under your contract. All kinds of problems can arise, and you must write your contract in a way that provides an escape route when such problems come up. Remember though, if you are excessively careful and try to put too many escape clauses into the deal, your seller is likely to lose interest.

5. Develop a stable of buyers. Your buyers are the key to your success in the wholesaling business. You want to continually be building your list of interested real estate investors. When your list is big enough, all you have to do is an email blast to find a buyer quickly. You may even be so lucky as to find yourself the beneficiary of a bidding war between buyers. Keeping good records of the types of properties your buyers are interested in can make you into one of their favorite sources, and can be the key to a very successful career in wholesale.

6. Closing the deal. Once you have found the right buyer, and negotiated the sale of the contract, you simply drive to your title company's office and complete the deal. This is usually about assigning the contract to the buyer, although sometimes dual closings can be a good way to complete a wholesaling deal This means one closing between you and the seller, and, immediately, another closing between you and the buyer.

7. Deposit your cash. This was fun, wasn't it? You brokered the deal, collected your fee, and now all you have to do is deposit your money. If you've done a good job, your deposit may be substantial. This whole process can be fun, and it is an exciting

way to make a lot of money in real estate with very little of your own cash in the deal. All this takes is knowledge, ingenuity, and courage.

Understanding Wholesaling: a view from 30,000 feet.

Wholesaling is a way to move product from one owner to another. In the real estate industry, the product is not something that you actually transport from place to place, then warehouse it for resale. The product in the real estate business is property, so the only thing that literally changes hands are documents and money, and even those are electronic these days.

Because there's nothing to pick up and deliver, you can actually wholesale real property with no money of your own. You take control of a property by putting it under contract.

And then, you have the rights to that property, so you find the person who would want to buy it. What you make as a profit is the spread in the middle. Sometimes that can be a lot of money, sometimes a little, but you basically can get into the wholesaling arena for no money whatsoever.

FIX AND FLIP

This book is about thinking like, and becoming an investor. Fixing and flipping is really not about becoming an investor. As I have clearly discussed in other chapters of this book, there are many benefits to be a real estate investor, including cash flow, capital gains, equity build-up by having your renters pay off your mortgage for you, equity build-up from appreciation, and tax savings.

Of these, the only one available to flippers is capital gain.

At one time, as a kid, I made some very good money flipping, but as I discussed elsewhere in this book, I realized that I was leaving enormous amounts of money on the table. Finding the deals was very valuable, but took a lot of ingenuity and work. So, once I had done that part of it, I decided for myself that I really wanted to get more out of the deals I found.

As a house-flipper, you will buy, rehab, and sell the property as quickly as possible to avoid months of carrying costs. These carrying costs include monthly bills like financing charges, property taxes, condo fees (if applicable), utilities, and any other maintenance bills required to keep the house in good physical or financial standing.

Flipping is not a passive business activity. Instead, it's a day job. An investor who stops flipping stops bringing in any money until they find and flip their next house.

On the other hand, flipping can help pay your day-to-day bills and to prop up other investments financially.

House flippers need to know about rehab costs, planning, and similar skills. If you already have some of that kind of experience, it's a huge plus, but you can even buy a software package to calculate time and expenses.

Estimating rehab costs is key. Being good at estimating rehab costs (or getting better at it) is an investment worth making.

Flipping real estate properties is one of the most lucrative professions on earth. But, just like the other highly lucrative professions, there is a lot to know. You can spend many years learning, and still find new mistakes to make.

Attempting to jump in and create a career as a fixer/flipper without taking the time to study and to become highly proficient could be a very expensive lesson for you. I will not waste our time telling you about the horror stories of people who were lured into trying to do fix and flip deals without knowing what they were doing, but rest assured those stories exist, and you do not want to be one of them.

I am not going to attempt to give you a shortcut course on fixing and flipping real estate. This would be a project that could take me years, and it would be a disservice to you.

There are wonderful institutions, organization and groups focused on fixing and flipping. If this is a profession you choose to pursue, I encourage you to do so.

While you are studying, learning and practicing, you can enter the real estate business, make great money, and create a great life for yourself while you are learning the fix and flip profession. Many of the ideas you will pick up in this book will be a wonderful place for you to start your journey.

Taking over existing financing

This is an enormously valuable skill, which is not that difficult to acquire. In your travels, as you seek deals, you will find real estate owners who are in trouble for one reason or another. Learning to find them is only the beginning. However, the deal involves helping them to get out of trouble by acquiring their property, taking over their existing mortgages.

This is an almost secret investing model that has made many millionaires, over just a few years, without either credit or huge savings.

OTHER IMPORTANT DECISIONS YOU MUST MAKE

Choosing location

I generally bought properties where I was because it fit my preference to buy and hold things that were tangible to me. Being in the same area and being able to visit the homes myself, made them that much more real to me.

So, I would like to buy a lot in zip codes near each other because that would make my management easier.

Other considerations that would come into play for me could include scaling the property management end of it, meaning I could rely on the same crew and keep those people working.

Some areas are better for real estate investment than others, obviously, so the growth and development in an area is one of the factors that you'd look at when you're going to invest: is the population is obviously increasing as in Colorado, Florida, and Texas compared to the midwestern states facing the future with diminishing populations? Is a major new employer coming to town or a growth industry budding? Chasing economic development in the belief the infrastructures will usually follow makes sense if you can beat the crowd in.

Take a place where Amazon is planning to put up a distribution center, or the region is opening a new commercial park or a business incubator. A lot of the times the rent may not be that high at right now, but you're expecting that when the area becomes more attractive, you're going to be able to raise the rent. And so, you might take a lower return on equity right now because you're looking for the future.

It seems obvious to me, but it is worth mentioning that the growth and development in an area is one of the factors to consider when choosing your location. For example, the population is obviously increasing as in Colorado, Florida, and Texas compared to the midwestern states facing the future with diminishing populations? Is a major new employer coming to town or a growth industry budding? Following, and even better, anticipating economic development in the belief the infrastructure build-out will usually follow, makes sense if you can beat the crowd in strategic business choices:

As I went through the process of building a business, the rate of return was not always the main thing I looked at initially. Having a bunch of properties in one area that will be managed by one person, ultimately paying down the mortgages so, at some point, they'd all be free and clear is the way that I built my business, not based on some of the factors that a passive investor would be looking at.

You could simply wait and raise the rent, or it would actually make it easier, in a competitive situation, to lower your rent because you have a lower interest rate and a lower basis. You'd have the flexibility to actually lower your rent to beat your competition. If you'd bought all the properties for cash, and the market got tight and it was hard to rent, you could have the lowest rents on the block and still be getting some return.

Moreover, an Amazon or a company like that is going to build an infrastructure around it. So, you would think appreciation would be happening in that marketplace too because of the supply and demand over the course of the next ten years, there probably be more demand than supply.

Full time or part time?

As one who has had to begin with nothing multiple times, I have a piece of advice for the beginning investor, whether your business is going to be real estate or something else: keep your day job. This is not a defeatist attitude. It's just practical math.

You have a built-in advantage over a full-time investor because you don't have to be able to lift the cash. Also, you can reinvest all the profits, and it's easier for you to start getting bank financing before you have a lot of assets because your stable income from work can help you early in your career.

On the other hand, some just make up their mind and take the plunge. Take the island, burn the ships, you know the all-in attitude, burn the ships and go all in, like Dane Peterson who works with me. He worked for Bank of America for seven years or something. He planned his exit, calculated when, then, he quit his job. Most people have a little bit more fear and a little bit more calculating and want to test the waters first. And so, you can start little by little. You can start anywhere you want. Start investing in real estate and building a rental portfolio while you're working. And once you get up to a place where your passive income is comfortable enough for you to quit, you can leave your job, going in all the way. You can proceed little-by-little, learn how to wholesale properties, learn how to buy, fixing and flip. If you're a handyman and you want to work weekends and you actually want to work on your house, work on a weekend and at night.

Rich or poor? It is your choice. Pick one now!

We all learn from early childhood on, that money is not everything, and that money is not the secret of happiness. We all know about rich people who have life difficulties, divorces, crime and every possible type of misery. But let me share the lesson I have learned over my nearly

7 decades of life. I have been poor, and I have been rich. Rich is definitely more fun.

Trading Time for Money

Today, there is a story going around that the economy is set up for the rich, and that everyone else is left behind. In America, nothing could be further from the truth.

Throughout this book, I talk about the mental game of life, and the fact that your thoughts determine what kind of life you lead.

Poor people grow up believing that the way to participate in the economy is to learn to sell your time for money. They believe that the way to improve your life is to get better at selling your time for money. The truth is, the most valuable thing you have is your time, and everything can be replaced except time.

The rich teach their children that the objective in this money game is to use your capital to buy other people's time. As they get older and better at the game, they learn that the ideal solution is to buy other people's time, with OTHER PEOPLE'S MONEY.

There is no better place to do that than the real estate business.

Banks love to lend money on real estate, and they spend more money seeking real estate deals to lend on than they spend on anything else.

If you can get over your shyness and acquire some confidence, you will find that the people in your life also feel very comfortable investing in real estate. Finding a lender or investor for a good real estate deal is easier than finding money for just about anything else.

Hard money

If credit is hard to find, or you have a deal that just can't wait for traditional financing, the Internet is full of advertisements and articles talking about hard money. If you are going to be in real estate, one of the things you're always going to want available to you is cash. Assuming you haven't been able to secure financing with banks or lines of credit at today's rates, but you want to play the game, hard money comes from many different sources.

Companies that loan money quick, charge a high-interest rate, typically. If you pay one point on a loan of $100,000 that's $1,000 for getting the money, but hard money is usually about two points and twelve percent interest right now. As you become a better investor and work that hard money connection, you should be able to get lower and lower rates as you become a safer calculated, consistent client.

When I, when I started my real estate career, a guy loaned me money at ten percent interest, and I was happy to get it. The formula worked for me. I could make money; he was making money. And we developed a relationship. Now, if I were to borrow from him, it's five percent and no points, no questions asked.

I needed to find the money so I needed to find a partner. There are techniques for getting out there and finding people who have the money and want to buy deals. Even when I didn't know any people, I got around. Early on, I had a job at a bar so I could meet people and I had an active mouth and I had a desire, so I talked to everybody.

Most people like to talk about making money so if you can get their attention and make us short, quick presentation, that's powerful enough to get them to pay attention to what you're talking about. It's called the Elevator Pitch because it should be quick enough to deliver it while you're riding on an elevator. Write it out, memorize it like it was a poem and practice it in front of a mirror, even if it makes you feel stupid. It will make you feel smart when you deliver it for real. It just has to be something that you believe in it enough to convey your enthusiasm, your conviction about what you're doing, so other people will want to buy your dream.

Hard Money – paying for convenience

Using hard money actually takes away the time constraint because hard money should be available to you immediately when you find a deal. But it makes it a little bit more challenging if you're flipping a property because of the interest rate that you're paying. So, if you borrow hard money and you haven't bought a really good deal, or you're not good at what you're doing and you don't know how to manage your crews, then it takes a long time to see a return on your investment, then the interest rate you pay for hard money could be a hindrance.

The right mentor makes everything easier and increases your chances of success 100-fold.

If you can find a mentor, somebody to go work within your local marketplace that might take you under their wing, that can help you avoid any number of beginner's mistakes and costly pitfalls. Most of the time, successful people want to help people. Go look for a person in your local marketplace who's doing what you want and ask them if they'll help you. Over the years I've helped lots of people – anybody who would ask, I would basically help.

If we can learn from other people's mistakes or have a blueprint for success that other people have used, good, but you don't need them, and you don't need me; you just need yourself making a determination and setting your sights on a goal that you have, Nobody can stop a guy who's going to where he's going, and nobody can help a guy who's a quitter. So, as somebody's going to get into this business, make up your mind that you're going to not fail, that no matter what, you're going to forge forward until you find the right information and to keep on going until you're successful.

I oftentimes mentor people who make themselves valuable. They may do an internet website or they may do cold calling. They look for wholesaling opportunities, things that are valuable in return for mentoring them. You might be able to get a very good mentor by finding a way to be valuable. I've been very fortunate that people have noticed me and that I'm willing to help. I've had people over the last months, years step up to just come around to learn. In turn, they've offered me things that they're good at, that I'm not as a natural exchange, I'm a giver, too. So, if you're going to give me something, I'm going to give back. Anybody who has reached a level of success is a giver in life because to really be successful in life, you've got to give and you've got to grow.

I would really highly recommend that you use this as a way to get into the business with some guidance. Go find a guy who's doing what you want to do and offer him something that may be valuable to him and try to get into their world. And they're out there because generally speaking, I find that the more successful somebody is, the more they're willing to help and give.

On the other hand, people who are marketing online are doing that for a business, and generally, *that's* their main business. So, the people you're going to find marketing online are selling seminars or selling coaching or selling programs you can buy for *them* to make money. There are a lot of people professing to have a lot of knowledge and experience, but all they know how to do is market themselves well, and how to put information into a formula to sell to other people.

They look really slick. They sound really good, *and they have some really good information*, but they don't have the nuts and bolts expertise because they haven't done it themselves. Until you get into the field until you've actually done these things, you really don't know all the obstacles and you don't know how to overcome all the obstacles. Although in the end, he who uses most resources, wins.

Having a mentor will shorten your learning curve and give you direction. Or, you can hire a coach. In some cases, a coach can become a mentor. If somebody hires me for a coach, ultimately, I'll probably become their mentor. But a mentor can just be somebody that you look up to who can give you, life guidance or real estate guidance or coaching in the direction of what you want to have and that, that doesn't have to cost money.

Many people get stuck in that loop of just gathering information, analysis, part paralysis as you said. If you're going to do this, just jump in, go find the mentor, go find the coach, go find the direction. Go get started. You'll learn everything that you need to learn about the industry and about your life and about how to live as you embark on an endeavor that could lead you to a life of fulfillment, happiness, and financial freedom.

Learn as you go, as we say, because you're never going to have all the information that's going to take you and go get started. Take the first step.

The first and most important skill to learn is how to identify properties and find deals. When you learn how to find deals, everything becomes available to you. You can wholesale them, fix them and flip them, or you can turn them into rental properties. So, the first thing to do is make a decision that you want to learn how to find deals.

I'm generally not one of the "cap-rates" guys. The capitalization rate is simply the ratio of a rental property's net operating income to its purchase price plus any other upfront expenses. It is the accepted, standardized formula for measuring the profitability of a deal vs. the price you pay to buy in. This type of valuation tool is important in comparing one investment with another. It is precisely analogous to the price/earnings ratio which is the standard for measuring the relative value of a company vs. another company.

Numbers, for me, aren't everything. Profitability is a good place to start, but, for me, lifestyle factors also matter. How easy is the property to manage? Is it located near my other properties? How does it fit into my current business? Reliability of income is crucial to me, because I want as close as possible to a hassle-free life.

The Math of Investing: Capitalization Rates

If you bought a $100,000 house and you're making $10,000 a year after expenses, after the taxes and maintenance, borrowing eighty percent of the money to purchase it, then you're really making above twenty percent a year on your actual cash investment.

It's very hard to equal that with another investment with income as stable as safe as rental real estate.

That is not to say that relying on cap rates is a bad investment strategy, it's just not mine. In fact, understanding cap rates and how to use them as a tool is worthwhile in its own right.

Capitalization rates are computed with the assumption a property is bought for cash, so you can look at the value, independent of how it's financed, which gives you a handy yardstick to compare different properties for potential deals.

Beyond a simple ratio, a cap rate is a measure of risk. The theory is, a higher cap rate, the riskier an investment is, and so, a lower cap rate means a less risky investment. It works just like investing in stocks and bonds. As a general rule, you get a lower rate of return on short term bonds than long term because you are risking your money for less time, Longer-term bonds have higher yields because you are betting over more years' time, increasing the uncertainty and, therefore, risk. Risk is your best estimate of the chance that you are going to break Warren Buffet's First Law of Investing: Don't lose money. A good investor does not stop at paying attention to ROI but also learns to factor in the risk involved and prepare for the worst-case scenarios.

Positioning for Safety

I started my real estate career both times with multifamily housing because of the income. This investment just felt safer to me. You'd have at least two tenants to pay off one mortgage and if one went away at least you'd have some money coming in. Generally speaking, you will be getting higher rent for the amount of money you invested - a higher cap-rate.

Commonly, people start out buying single-family homes because that's just what they're used to. Single family homes are easy to find, and they are easy to finance.

But they don't produce as much income, and if a single unit becomes vacant, you're getting no income at all. A multifamily property, of four units and below, can qualify for the same kind of financing as a signle family home, but it can produce more cash flow and you can find economies of scale. After all, the same property manager can handle one tenant or four.

I just happened to like multifamily houses because, in general, you earn more income from them for each dollar invested in purchasing the property.

As a matter of fact, most of my portfolio now is multifamily and small apartment complexes because those give you more income per dollar invested, and per time and energy invested.

From ten to twenty or so units is a sweet spot for me. That's really too small for real estate investment trusts to bother with, and it's too big for most beginners.

It's important to know that real estate is only a tool.

What really matters and determines your level of success is how you live your life. You're going to be a successful real estate investor when you get your mindset right and you move in the direction of what you want each and every day. The key point is to get started, right now. Take the first step of making some goals for yourself. Decide what your priorities are. Take some action each day in service to those priorities and create the life of your dreams. Everybody has their own gift. And when they figure out, what it is and how to use it in the direction that they're going in their lives, it becomes a special opportunity to become more.

The stories that we tell ourselves are truly powerful because they determine what we think we are capable of doing. And, whether you think you can or think you can't, you're right. We can change the stories that we've told ourselves, and we can decide to create a story that will move us in the direction of anything we want. Moreover, there is a science and a system for doing it. It starts with growing your confidence. There are different kinds of confidence, the confidence that we get from how others see us, there is self-confidence and there's faith.

Confidence comes from the discipline to spend that time in an organized, focused manner. When you take your priorities in life seriously, and you constantly press yourself to make a slight improvement every single day, you begin to feel better about yourself and begin to build an unshakable foundation for our future. When you harmonize your actions and your thoughts and focus them on building your foundation for your life, you can build a skyscraper to live in.

You have to get through the obstacles. You kind of get through the disappointments. You've got to get through life's happenings. You've got to get through bad breaks. You've got to get through the market crash. You've got to get through people leaving. You've got to get through life. But if you've got a goal and a focus on yourself, discipline, nothing is in your way.

Take a mental course of action that consciously directs your thinking each and every day. That's the hard part. Once you've done that, it doesn't matter what you choose in life. When you've made up your mind and you push away the fears and memories of the past, you have a clear vision of what you are trying to do.

Financial Freedom

Wealth is being able to do what you want when you want, where you want. In my opinion, if you want to build wealth and financial freedom, the pointers in this book are a great place to start.

When you find a path that appeals to you, read everything you can get your hands on, about it. You have the ability to become one of the world's foremost experts on one narrow subject. Do that now, this month. Start today and continue your studies until you really know exactly what you are doing.

I've done that through income-producing real estate, whether it's single, family homes, multifamily homes, small apartment complexes, mobile homes and things like that.

We always come back to the mental game

What Your Real Estate Business Plan Should Include

Having determined your strategy for building your real estate business, starting with figuring out which aspects of the business actually appeal to you, you next should focus on formulating your plan. Just as every campaign needs a battle plan, every startup requires a well thought out business plan. This is a critical step, both because bankers, investors and even family members that you ask to back you will demand to see one, but because recognizing and identifying what you want to accomplish is the first step to achieving it.

Your business plan may be structured and formatted in a number of ways, but they should all include some common elements:

Mission Statement – This is a clear, straightforward statement of purpose that includes the benefits to investors and the public at large that you expect your business to provide. Read a few corporate and non-profit organizations' mission statements to get a feel for how one should sound.

Goals – What do you hope to achieve? How long are you giving yourself to make progress toward it? How will real estate help you get there? Write that down. There are no wrong answers. Your goals can change over time, in fact, they really ought to, either because you are well on your way to achieving them or, if not, they may need to be reevaluated. Be sure to include both short- and long-term goals. By getting as surpassing the smaller, initial goals, you'll boost your self-confidence and help you stay motivated.

Strategy – This one should be easy because you've already figured out what your strategy is – it's the choices you made when deciding what you hoped to end up with and what ways you are most comfortable pursuing.

Timeline – Along with defining your goals, you'll want to give some thought to how long you have to make those dreams come true. That will, of course, be dependent on your initial circumstances – are you starting out in life, do you have family and other commitments that you have to factor in? How much worry or risk are you ready to handle? Will you have the resources you will need to sustain you for as long as it might take?

Market – Describe what you're looking for, whether you're fixing and flipping or looking for passive income, single-family, townhouse or apartment complex? Essentially, it's the same question you've had to answer to figure out what side of the business you want to participate in. As a beginner, backers will expect you to stay within an area you are familiar with, and likely a property a short distance from where you live and work. That way, you can gain experience and become expert, analyzing deals and opportunities in your own neighborhood first. At the same time, you can get to know the players in your area, which will ultimately help you find partners and even more opportunities.

Parameters – Along with knowing what end of the business you're venturing into, you have to know your limits, and so do the people you are hoping to work with and back your efforts. What will your loan-to-value and cash-flow requirements be? What are your budgets for the initial purchase price, for the rehabbing, your timeline for completing the project and what your expectations are for the sale price? One of the most important lessons anyone learns in this business is to stick to your numbers, no matter what. There should be no deal that you cannot walk away from if it doesn't meet your criteria.

Financing – How do you plan to pay for deals? Are you using conventional loans, hard money, private money, equity partners, seller financing, lease options, or some other creative financing method?

Exit Strategies – What is your endgame? Are you going to turn a property to make a quick profit or hold it for income and let it appreciate to make a profit? As I mentioned earlier, what is your worst-case scenario – what are your alternatives if the market flattens or unanticipated expenses appear? Make sure to carefully document your income and expenses, and prepare for the unexpected. Have a series of exit strategies in case the first one, or the third doesn't work out as planned.

If the end goal is financial freedom, it not only matters where you are at what point you've reached in your life but also at what stage in your investing life are you?

I'm 60. I don't have a ten-year or twenty-year plan to start building rental properties, making $100 a month and paying down our mortgage. But Dane or some of the young guys that I like to work with, can make a plan with building and buying standalone properties in specific areas with a longer time horizon. When we talk about age difference or people starting young and making a business plan to get financially free with the vehicle of real estate, we're talking a ten-year process for sure, forget three years.

Don't get caught up in the emotion of investing, whether it's real estate or stocks and bonds, or even precious metals – maybe especially precious metals because they especially appeal to the emotional side. Following your emotions in investing is really just following the crowd. People like to agree with other people, it's hard-wired into our brains. Back on the savanna a half-million years ago, getting along with the gang was a better survival strategy than insisting you're right. And the more people running in one direction, the stronger the pull to run with them. After all, they can't all be wrong, right?

The emotional side is like, "Oh, the market's stinks right now." Like in 2008. Everybody was going through foreclosures or short sales, and they thought their lives were falling apart and they allowed themselves to be carried away by emotion.

Ever hear the adage, buy on the bad news and sell on the good? When prices are falling and the majority of investors are racing to find a way out is an excellent time to make long term business investments, especially rental property investments. Just as at any other time, invest the time and brainpower to be certain *this* deal pencils out even when the crowd feels as though it is temporarily right.

When you've made a business plan, you've got to stay the course. Yes, you've got to have the strength, courage and determination to stick to your plan and ignore the blaring headlines. When we're talking about financial independence via rental real estate, it doesn't matter if the economy's good or bad. Tenants still need a place to live.

You're going to buy property that's going to put cash in your pocket while you are paying down the mortgages. Regardless of the economic climate at the time, you are consistently growing financially.

How to Get Started with Little or No Money – Yes, you can do this!

To the handyman:

First, I want to take a moment to speak to that rare person who has a construction background, or who is a real handyman or likes hands-on projects. You may want to start with a house that you can actually practice on. Learn the ins and outs of buying, fixing and selling. You can start on a shoe-string, and with sufficient effort you can find yourself a partner who has a little money, and is looking for a chance to use his capital to profit from your time. I can tell you from long experience that people with money need you.

Learning to create and sell win-win situations is a skill that will carry you anywhere you want to go in life.

I can promise you, that if you are a skilled carpenter, plumber or handyman, people with money, who wish to benefit from your efforts are joining up you at this moment. The only thing you are missing is the confidence to go out and put the deal together with that money partner who is eagerly waiting for you.

No construction skills and no money? No problem! Opportunity awaits you!

If you don't have any money, it's obvious that a good place to start is wholesaling. This simply means using your ingenuity to find the deals for the people who have the resources to do them. For starters, without money, it's difficult to bring in someone to work on maintenance and repairs, but with effort, skill and experience, you can learn to be great at finding the deals and profitably handing them off to the people with the resources.

One of the houses that I'm rehabbing now came from a wholesaler in my favorite market who has a different niche than mine. His team goes out and works with real estate agents and gets the listings out of their pocket listings – listings that haven't made it to the mainstream yet. This particular house had a structural problem – a foundation issue, and the porch was kind of sinking. Houses with structural problems or a house that had a fire in it are a little more demanding to work on. Because this house had a structural problem, many people will it because they think it's too difficult to deal with So, they brought it to me, and I partnered with them.

Getting into a real estate deal is one thing but making a profit means having a way out – an exit strategy - as well. I always want to know my worst-case scenario. What will my exit strategy be?

If I plan on buying a particular house today and flipping it, but by some chance, the economy went into a decline or something unforeseen happened, my worst-case scenario could be to keep it as a rental property.

At this point in my life, I'm not really buying any properties unless they drop in my lap and fit a particular model. For example, if it's on a street or in a subdivision where I own other properties.

I generally stick to deals to accommodate my students or partners. I put myself in their shoes and ask myself, were I at their stage of life, would I would buy it? If so, I'll probably partner with them.

I do love to collaborate and get involved with people doing syndications or buying bigger deals, but I don't buy too many properties by myself, right now. And there are a number of reasons why. For me, my age makes a difference.

BUILDING A TEAM TO SUCCEED

Real estate provides an opportunity for all kinds of people. Some people are salespeople, some people are organizers. Some people work with others well, some don't.

You have got to find your niche inside the niche of real estate. We're talking about wholesaling, flipping or earning passive income to rent the properties; different kinds of people are obviously better at different aspects, and you would want to master each one of them if you want to do it all. The beauty of building an organization = actually, building a business =the key to success is to find the people who have the skills that you don't.

Where you start will depend on the people you recruit, who are good at what you're not best at. No one succeeds entirely on their own anymore, if they ever did. The story of the self-made millionaire is a myth.

Not that you don't have yourself to thank for what you accomplish, in real estate and in life, but there are always people you need, and expertise you don't have. Moreover, you've got neither the time nor the smarts to master every aspect of everything you need to do. Finding the people who give you information that you could have gotten on your own *is finding it on your own,* but doing it the smart way.

To really be successful, you are going to have to assemble your team. Everything starts with building teams, unifying people and organizing them to work together. Real estate investing can be a very lonely business and you can only go so far on your own. Create teams and include as many people as possible, because that's the way that we actually make our lives better, while making the world a better place.

I always try to recruit talents and special skillsets I don't have – people who may think and hunt for things differently from me.

The way I operate in all endeavors is to hire the best I can, develop friendships with them and trust them to lead me to new opportunities. I especially need someone who is great at tax strategies on my team, and so do you.

Laws change all the time, particularly in real estate, and those changes can come from every level of government, from the feds down to the local zoning commission or planning agency. The benefits you can achieve through real estate are ever-changing.

Don't try to do it on the cheap. I learned that the hard way, as I learned most of my lessons. When the economy was crashing and I thought I was going broke, I switched my accountant to somebody much less expensive. Sometimes, you get what you pay for –'nuff said? You always want the best tax accountant, the best real estate attorney and the best advisors you can afford. You can bet your competitors will have the best they can find.

I put people to work in many different sectors: sales, leadership, maintenance, rehabbing, landscaping, air conditioning and heating, all kinds of people and companies. One of the reasons I didn't quit and just shut it down over the last years when I was not really active in the business, was because I felt committed to all the families of the people who have been depending on me for business all these years. I've got people who have been with me ten and twenty years, and' therein lies the magic in the whole thing. All that love is a big part of what makes this whole engine run. There's a deep sense of community, family, trust, and love.

Everything's about creating and supporting teams. Everything's about building teams, unifying people and organizing people to work together. I have some areas in which I am exceptional and that are different from other people's gifts.

I've been able to figure out how to teach the leaders in my organization to recognize people's gifts and then figure out how they learn. And when you combine those two things together, you can create magic in each individual's life. It is really very gratifying, and more important to me than all the money we make.

Over the decades, I have started a number of companies in businesses other than real estate, as well. Almost always by partnering, and building a team. That way, I could focus on the parts of the business I excelled at and leave the things I did less well than someone else, to them.

Back in those days, I was called a dream maker because I used to say, "Go find the person with a dream and bring them to me. Find a person with a dream, introduce me, and let's go - let's rock and roll." And that's kind of what I'm doing now. I find the person with a dream. My dream is so big right now that anybody's dream can fit inside it. I can flesh it out quickly enough and see if there's synergy there, to make our dreams come true together.

Building your team begins with building yourself. You cannot build an effective team unless you have the right values, integrity, and formula to turn yourself into someone who can lead a team. You lead by exemplifying the qualities that your group will expect from your team members. If you want a team to be competent with integrity and be accountable, you'd better be competent and accountable. And, you have to transmit a unique vision, something that can inspire your team toward constant improvement.

I also want to let them know how much I care about them, and to always keep my commitments, and, especially, to let them know if they do their thing, they'll never have to worry about the money. I let them know they don't just work for me. We work together.

I want everything I'm doing with anyone to be a collaboration, or a partnership or a co-mingling of the minds and money. I did that from the start, and I continue working this way with my team. I just want my circle to get bigger, I want to help people, and the more people who get involved, the stronger and more successful we become

In many cases, you may meet a guy who has some analytic or computer skills but doesn't know how to evaluate real estate. Still, he has skills and he's resourceful in ways that you are not.

I look for people who are clearly not like me. I look for people who have complementary skills and want to make money in real estate. I find the guy who's really skilled in computers, who wants to get into tax delinquencies or tax liens. I know there's a lot of money to be made there, but I don't have the time, patience, energy or desire to really dig into that arena. So, I find somebody with the right skills, with the right leadership, who wants to exploit that opportunity, and he gets resourceful and finds out everything about that niche to create an income stream. Almost all my deals are like that. They're coming from other people who are looking at different techniques, exercising different skills and adding to our organization.

You're going to need a good management team, as well.

You're going to have to have a lot of good people. Develop people who can love to take care of the properties, as well as love to find new opportunities, and folks who just love to keep the business running smoothly.

Real Estate can be a roller coaster ride – ask anybody who was in the apartment market in the mid-1980s or almost any kind of real estate in 2008. But I weathered those storms and so did many other savvy investors. How? You keep your head straight as you're building your rental portfolio and building up your cash reserves.

Contrary to the very popular opinion that you must time the market, I have found that you can be successful in any part of the cycle, as long as the properties you acquire fit your needs. In fact, bad times are often the best time to buy.

Then, if you've got an infrastructure, a team in place, be it a management team or people with the know-how for building and doing things, when the cycle reverses and things are moving up again, you have the ways and means to jump in and capitalize when others can't or won't. When the market inevitably comes back, you're organized to take advantage of the opportunity.

We've already touched on some elements of a successful real estate team. Here, I want to give you a bullet-point list of the roles you will want to fill to make sure you have all the expertise you need.

A mentor – as I said some ways back, having someone who has done these things before, who can help guide you and save you from making the same mistakes she did, and show you the ropes, is an invaluable resource. If you can't find a partner or employer to take you under their wing, try hiring a coach.

A mortgage broker – You will want to develop relationships with the people who will supply you with financing. Virtually everything you will do in the real estate business (or most others, for that matter) are going to need investment at some point. If you have a bank loan officer or a mortgage lender ready to do business with you, you stand ready to jump on a new deal, and even to offer cash terms because you have the financing arranged in advance.

A real estate attorney – People proverbially all hate lawyers until they need one. And need one you will. A good lawyer is not only looking out for your interest in every deal you hope to make, but they are also the guardian of your good reputation, an advisor who can lead you to opportunities you might have overlooked, and who can warn you when you may be approaching a legal cliff. Keep in mind, attorneys can be compensated with a percentage of the profits, or whatever creative you can come up with. This is also a sales job, but one skill well worth developing.

A real estate and tax accountant – Once you start your business, not only do bookkeeping and taxes become more complicated - things any good CPA can handle - your numbers person should also be well aware of the ins and outs of real estate. Ideally, they will own properties of their own and can help you through the write-offs. A good tax accountant will save you much more than the cost of their service. Count on it.

An escrow officer or title rep – in a number of states, escrow officers or a title company will be acting as an intermediary in the deal, conducting a title search to make sure the property is free and clear of liens or other obligations, and as the person responsible for closing the deal. Having this person on your team helps assure that process proceeds quickly and smoothly. As always, you want people to look out for your interests.

An insurance agent – Pardon the expression but, Duh. No homeowner worth his salt would consider doing without insurance, and neither should you. Fire, flood, earthquake insurance should all be at the top of the list (and, yes, there are some major earthquake faults in the Midwest and South, not just in California and Alaska). Be sure to have her explain all the fine print, including exclusions and "force majeure" clauses. Having an insurance agent on your side can help avoid costly surprises if you ever do have to file a claim.

A real estate agent or broker – While we're on the subject of the obvious, you'll want access to the myriad tools that realtors and brokers have on hand that are unavailable to the general public. Then, too, there are plenty of details that an agent is in the business of handling on a daily basis. Of course, you can do what I did and start out by getting a real estate license. It can even be your day job for a while, a way to begin making money in real estate before you strike out on your own, while you learn the ins and outs of trading in real property.

Assuming you are interested in income-producing properties, and not just trading, either as a wholesaler or a quick-seller, you are going to want people who can help maintain the property. In that case, these team members are essential (unless you intend to do all the work yourself):

A general contractor – If you are buying a building that needs any kind of repairs or improvements, a good, trustworthy and reliable contractor can make your project. By the same token, a cut-rate contractor who does less than excellent work can cost far more than getting it done right in the first place. Protect yourself by hiring only a licensed, bonded, and insured contractor, and one with a reputation for getting the job done on time and under budget. A word to the wise – doing your research here will pay off in spades. Don't be lazy, and don't be cheap.

A handyman or caretaker – Just as a competent contractor is essential for the big jobs, the smaller, routine and day-to-day concerns that make all the difference to your tenants need to be taken care of promptly and efficiently. Even if you can handle the majority of repairs, how many late-night calls over a burst water pipe or a similar minor catastrophe do you want to have to take?

A property manager – If you plan on investing anywhere beyond your immediate vicinity, there has to be someone nearby who can handle things for you. Even if all your investments are in your own area, assuming you are intent on growing your business, there may be too many issues for you to juggle by yourself. A good property manager may be hard to find, but one that manages your rentals well will make your tenants happier and your life significantly easier. This one factor can make the difference between loving your real estate career and having it become a real burden.

Everybody has a gift. And when they figure out what it is and how to leverage it to move in chosen direction, it becomes a special opportunity to become more. When you ultimately make smart decisions and promises to yourself that move you in the direction of becoming a better human being, then keep those promises, the process automatically raises your self-esteem, and this is a key ingredient that helps transport you to the life of your dreams.

Fear of rejection, or not trying for fear of failure is just a way to stand in your own way. You can overcome any fear by meeting the obstacle head-on and tackling it. I had already gotten over any fear of rejection when I was at 17 years old, selling knives door to door. I think that pretty much took care of that problem forever.

Find that thing you're passionate about, that lights a fire inside you hot enough to make you feel you must go for it or you burn up from the inside, out. When you are obsessed with where you're going and what you're doing, there are no obstacles that can stand in your way.

If you've decided to become a real estate owner, choose a niche, like rehabbing a run-down gem.

Find a house with a popped-out pool or with the septic tank needing replacement. Have somebody coaching you, get a mentor or if you love challenges, master learning by trial and error. The only way you're going to get into the arena where you buy houses with popped up pools or fire damage or porches caving in or sinkholes - any of the things that scared most of the world - is to go into the deals and figure the way out. As I said, he who is most resourceful wins.

No matter how you acquire a property, as long as you buy it right, all you have to do is keep pushing through and getting to the finish line.

Whatever success I have had, was mostly done by figuring solutions on my own.

When I look back at my life, I really never had many real estate mentors. I read the books and I listened to the tapes. But there was no one person who showed me exactly what to do in real estate. It was me just gathering knowledge, getting hungry and wanting to find out more so I could be intelligent about what I was trying to do.

You find a way to get yourself in it. You take the plunge. You buy a property. You just focus and get it done. At the beginning, if you don't have a mentor and you're not smart about what you're doing, you may take some lumps. The people who make mistakes at first, but stay in the game and keep going, are the ones who really reap the great rewards and build something real that can sustain them for a very long time.

Perseverance is realizing that you're going to be able to win eventually. . Nick Bollettieri, the great tennis coach tells the story of Bjorn Borg. He became number one in the world, by a single conviction. He knew he was going to be the last one to get the ball over the net. That is all he had to know.

He did not know exactly what he was going to do every step of the way. You may not know how your plan will unfold. You may find out your initial strategy is simply not working. You may have to modify it or even switch to a different strategy. What you know in your heart of hearts is that you will not stop. You are completely confident because you know you will not stop. That means, instead of being motivated by fear, you are playing for love of the game. What a wonderful life that knowledge helps to create for you.

You don't stop, you go get it. Nothing stops you, and when you install that certainty inside you, you become unstoppable. You work through the obstacles. You get through the disappointments. Things happen in life, and you simply can't through them. You've got to get through bad breaks, the market crashing, people leaving. If you've got a goal and a focus on yourself, have the knowledge that you will never give up, nothing - no obstacle can standin your way.

Consciously directing your thinking each and every day is the takes practice - a lot of it. Once you've mastered that skill and know-how to execute through a systematic approach, it doesn't matter what you choose in life, as long as you've made up your mind and you've gotten your focus on a clear vision of what you want. When you push away the fears and memories of the past and you have a clear vision of with what you trying to do, you consciously get up and direct your thinking. At that point, you can accomplish anything. Direct your thinking and focus on what you want. Then, get in the arena, whether it's writing and publishing books, or creating a team, or building your real estate empire.

The fact that you picked up this book and the fact that you've gotten this far, suggests you've already decided within yourself that you're a person who can do it, wants to do it, and will do it.

So, start a plan today that will lead you towards becoming a more productive member of our community, to give back more to the world. In the end, that's what we're all here to do, to become better.

How to Find Deals: Everything Starts with Great Ideas

Whether it's stock market or business, some hamburger business or some salad business or some real estate business. When you find a little niche, you have an opportunity to get rich. For instance, specialized areas in real estate: delinquent tax, sales, probate, eviction, whatever it is. The answer is the same: be creative, do your research and be resourceful.

Being in the business of real estate would be actively getting involved in up finding your own rental properties, flipping your own real estate or wholesaling real estate. And, there are many other ways to be in real estate. You can buy notes; you can loan money.

Because I enjoy the business of dealing with rental properties and because of my hands-on approach to life in general, my investments in real estate have been in my backyard.

I've happened to choose backyards that are appreciating because I want to live where things are going on – where there's plenty of action.

My circle has come from building close by where I live. When you are going to be in the business of real estate and actively involved, you want to do that where you live. The more convenient your setup, the more energy you have for productivity and the more enjoyable is your work Remember, this is your life.

That is not a strategy for a hand-off passive investor and who just wants to watch the money coming in. In that case, the most important ingredient is finding a competent, experienced, reliable manager to handle the day-to-day decisions and ongoing maintenance. If you objective is to simply clip coupons while your people do the work, I've found that nothing else really matters. In this case, the choices of location open up to include almost anywhere. Just be sure you do your homework – your due diligence – to make sure you know what you're getting into and what to expect.

Spend the time. Check out your prospective manager. No amount of checking is too much. Even hiring an investigator or subscribing to an online background check service isn't excessive.

What kinds of lawsuits or legal issues has this manager had?

Talk to tenants of properties they manage and find out if they are happy and getting the service you hope to offer.

If you're just looking for possibilities to have passive income, create the freedom you want in your life, you may be better served to find areas, where the economic conditions either provide for more appreciation or in the cash flow arena a better rate of return on your money.

Some older "Rust Belt" cities like Detroit are experiencing a renaissance of young professionals and artists moving in. But even there, knowing which neighborhoods are drawing attention, and which are likely to be the next up-and-coming communities can be the difference between riding the crest of the wave of new development or swept under by the currents.

In that case, you find somebody in a marketplace where you want to invest your money, or you find the person who's getting the returns that you want, and who you can trust, and you let him decide what markets to put you in. You then have a real estate advisor, like having a trusted financial advisor. What a difference this one component can make in your life!

The niches I've been involved in actively have been wholesaling, flipping and building a rental portfolio.

Ultimately, I started building a management team to manage rental properties, a financial team to loan money. As the business grew many different legs, I've had multiple income streams from the real estate game.

Whatever you hope to accomplish, anything you do in life, you first need to learn about it, to find the information. So, you're going to have to do some digging, whether it's about the single-family housing market or the duplex or small multifamily market, apartment communities or the mobile home market.

Everybody knows where to get information on anything now. It's called the internet. You can find everything about everything, but there is so much information about so many things, even finding out what you need to know has a learning curve attached.

Finding Opportunity

What does opportunity look like? It comes in all shapes and sizes; it can be a big house, a little house, an expensive house, or junky house. It can be any type of property, apartment, whatever.

Learn to find places where there is unrealized value of any kind.

I look for distressed property, vacant property, lawns growing untended, windows covered up, trash all over the place.

Go by a neighborhood that interests you on trash day and you can see where people are moving out. Scout out yard sales, eviction notices on doors, code violations, any signs of vacancies or squatters, or property in need of help. Those are opportunities.

Look for absentee owners by searching the property tax records – is the mailing address different from the address of the property?

The courthouse is clearly one source for this type of leads. Zillow is be another place. MLS, the Multiple Listings Service subscribed to by most real estate agents and brokers would be another place to find great opportunities, and your county tax records would be another place.

There are all kinds of data resources available now.

Personally, I spend my time looking at houses. That's what I teach my students to do, these days.

Just look at houses. Get to know neighborhoods.

I visited and checked out as many houses as possible. This is, by far, the best way to become an expert.

It all begins with taking some action – the journey of a thousand miles begins with a single step. You're going to make some mistakes. But that's not something to be avoided if you can learn from them so you don't keep repeating the same ones.

If you want to make fewer mistakes, hire a coach and have them hold your hand and show you what to do and then go to work. If you're committed to doing this business, go find the coach right out of the gate. Go find somebody who's going to pay attention to you. Go find somebody who's done what you want to accomplish.

But it doesn't matter what you know if you don't put it to work. Then, you're getting nowhere because you have not yet begun to move. If you go to work and don't know anything, but you're working on it and trying to constantly improve, you'll figure it out.

Of course, it's easy to say, "just get creative." If it were that simple, everybody would already be doing it. Success may not be something that everybody can have – after all, for everyone getting a better than average deal, someone on the other side of the transaction is getting less than they could have. However, success, in whatever terms you define it, whether it is monetary rewards or some other marker, is available to *anybody*.

So, here are some more specific suggestions. Strategies can be as simple as looking for lawn signs, newspaper classifieds, or their 21st-century replacement, Craigslist, internet marketers. Or look for free and clear properties in a depreciating economy. Even in a rising real estate market, there are willing sellers.

People who have owned their home for a couple of decades may be ready to trade up. A homeowner whose mortgage is a lot less than the value of his or her house has a significant equity position in the property that they may be looking for a way to tap into. This is something else to look for in the tax records. See when the sale was recorded and at the mortgage on the property, and how much the mortgage was when they bought the house. Then compare that to the current assessed value.

Real estate sites like Zillow and Redfin can be excellent sources of information about the surrounding communities where you are seeking deals. Amenities like parks and playgrounds, highly rated public schools and even crime statistics are to be found at a granular level. These days, you can learn almost as much from your desktop as you can driving around town. So, think about what you can achieve if you do both!

One of the trends in the current decade is the so-called empty-nesters. There are older people whose kids have moved on and find they no longer need a three or four-bedroom split level, and might want a condo in the city, instead. You know they've got equity in the property that they can use to start the next phase of their lives. I'd be going with people who want to cash out, then go back and see the ones who bought their places in 2000 or 2001, because even if they had a thirty-year mortgage, it's halfway paid down and the value of their home has been appreciating for the last ten years.

We find a lot of older landlords and have been successful at turning them into profitable deals. They simply get tired of doing what they've been doing and it's time to cash in and they're ready get out. A lot of these folks in their seventies and eighties have been grinding away for years. And, though some might find the idea a bit ghoulish, probate records and the obituary page of the local paper are also sources of leads, as are estate sales. These are actually win-win situations. You're helping yourself by helping them with the next phase of their lives. If there is a formula for being part of the genius of our American capitalist culture, it is THE WIN-WIN SITUATION.

If you're working in the marketplace, it's always a good strategy to connect with probate attorneys. In each case, they indicate that someone has passed away and, while that is a personal tragedy for the family and friends, it is also an opportunity waiting in the wings. Just be considerate and sympathetic, and they will probably be grateful that you came.

The same creativity should go for developing and structuring the deal. When you find the right opportunity property, whether your intent is to flip it, wholesale it, or my favorite – just keep it and collect rents forever - your job is to find a way to present that deal to a buyer or investor that will make it irresistible. Think like an investor!. When you find that target property, you contact the owner. There are a whole host of ways to make that contact: send them an email, mail a regular letter, make a phone call (reverse directories will often have the phone numbers listed by addresses), postcard, or a door hanger. When you find the lead you want to go after, . How motivated are you to contact that person, and how resourceful are you? If there is one lesson for you to carry forward by reading my book, it is that resourcefulness is the key to your success. Experience and knowledge will come. Resourcefulness is the difference between the winners and the also-rans.

Whatever type of houses you are looking for, the story is the same; how you find them, and how you negotiate may change. Each market may be a little bit different. There are internet companies that provide easier access to information I mentioned above, but the ones we rely on now may not even be around by the time this book comes out. In three years, some of the information in this book may have evolved; some of the lead source I'm giving you here may not even be working anymore. Still, the ideas and the means of finding real estate deals are the same You make a decision that that's what you're going after and you just keep digging. Make a decision to be absolutely relentless, and you are sure to win.

Remember, as well, that just because you find a productive vein of information online, that doesn't make that the only source or even the best source.

When you decide on your path of least resistance, that is likely to also mean that's where many resourceful people are hunting. The people who find niches and are resourceful, find ways to work a little bit differently. They seek out some different strategies - innovative ways to find some extra nuggets. You go mainstream or you may miss out on the obvious, but you also go side stream and try to dig up things that other people are less likely to discover before you.

There are plenty of opportunities in foreclosure, taxing, probates and all those kinds of sources of leads. Just decide. You're going to fully develop a business. I keep coming back to the main key to success that has worked for me and made me a millionaire many times over. Make the decision to be endlessly resourceful and totally relentless.

In every area of life when you become clear on what you want, you just do it, and never give up. Every time you come up against an obstacle of any kind, you neutralize it. You gain confidence and you know in your heart that obstacles make you stronger. Those obstacles lead to the home runs. Every time you learn this lesson, you're closer to your objective – transforming your life.

One Crucial Question: Where Are All The Rich People?

Hundreds of millions of manuals and how-to books on real estate, and on every other type of business, have been sold. Yet, there still are not very many really wealthy people in our country, or in the world for that matter.

There's a terrific reason for this, which has become clear to me in my seventh decade of life. The most important wisdom I can pass on to you is this: THE MENTAL GAME IS EVERYTHING!

The reason you're interested in me - or, the reason you should be interested in me and what I have to offer is that I've actually done what you want to do.

The issue is not how many houses I own; you want to be financially independent and powerful, take care of your kids and send them to good schools. You want to be able to solve all these life issues once and for all.

There are a number of excellent real estate books and manuals, which go into great detail about how to do every part of this, or any other industry.

As I said in the introduction, I don't know that the world needs another manual, and I'm not going to waste my time or yours duplicating the great how-to books that are already out there. The truth is, I learned most of what I know from those very resources. In fact, I'm including at the end of this book, an excellent list of resources. The smartest thing you could do is to study those books and manuals.

This is your chance to develop and protect the one factor that matters most - the one factor that does make people rich. I'm telling you that it's the mental game and what's inside that makes the difference. And it's not really how I fix roofs. It's about how I make decisions and follow through and connect to God - how I live my life and how you can learn to live your life. I can tell you, with complete certainty, that this book contains the true secret of being successful in real estate, or in anything else.

PART 3 – HOW YOU LIVE YOUR LIFE (B) THE LONGER VERSION

THE KEYS TO FREEDOM AND SUCCESS

Learning How to Learn to Be Effective

The first step for anyone is to figure out how we're going to stand up and determine to be the best we can be each day, moving in the direction of what we want in our life. This is something you may not have even known when you opened this book. But if you have opened this book, you at least suspect there's something in here to help you achieve the life you want.

Perhaps, you are attracted by the fact that I had made a lot of money, but now you know. By now, though, you know there is much more to this. You may choose to follow my path, or create your own. Either approach is just fine.

Right now, it's important to get clear on who you are, and what you are deciding you want in your life.

To start this process, take a few moments right now and write down exactly what has happened in your life in the past year. Include the events that have occurred, your accomplishments and also the changes in your beliefs, thoughts and objectives.

_____

_____

_____

_____

_____

_____

I began by making a list of my priorities and my goals – a vision of where I wanted to be and turned them into flashcards. The cards are the beginning of a process of impressing those images on your brain, to begin to activate a part of your brain that starts to take information and turn it into action.

The unconscious part of our brain doesn't know what's real and what's not real. So, if we can get a strong enough vision, and impress it upon our unconscious, it will treat that information as if it has actually happened. The process to follow would be repetition.

You have to repeat something over and over again to condition yourself subconsciously, and it is even more effective if you add images with emotion

It's like learning the ABC's when you're young. At the beginning, it requires effort until it has become a habit. Then your unconscious, the powerful part of your brain, takes over. Intellectual information is only five or ten percent of our thinking, and ninety percent of it is subconscious. So, we're going to have to get that subconscious in line with our creative, conscious thinking.

Make a decision and take action. Any productive movement, any action is good action. You're either growing or dying. You've got to make a decision that you're going to grow.

Then you start to take some more action and you'll start connecting different pathways in your brain. Recent discoveries have shown just how much the brain is reconstructing itself, changing and adapting, forming new neural pathways, the highways down which our thoughts and feelings are driven. We actually can get a lot smarter when we learn how we learn and apply that knowledge in the most important areas of our life.

A lot of people have never connected with the fact that the action they take actually makes a difference in what their life is. Their bodies are overcoming their minds.

First, know that your bodily feelings will be stronger than your mind until you take control of your mind and decide to rule your body. The day you take control of your mind to rule your body is the day things start to come together.

What does that day look like? Say, for instance, you're addicted to sweets – it's beyond a "sweet tooth." You say you're going to quit, and the next time some candy or ice cream is in front of you, you don't indulge.

That action begins to redirect your neural pathways, and just like a path gets worn from people walking on it, those new paths can get strengthened by repeated use. They get stronger and linked together with other positive thoughts and actions. Put an action plan together to move in the direction of your priorities and, at the same time, integrate some specific strategies in your life to get a little leverage in raising your conscious awareness.

So, if were that easy, wouldn't everybody be doing it? Yes. Everybody can, at least in theory. The fact of the matter is, it is simple, but it's not that easy. It's work. It requires diligence and effort, discipline and time, all things that most of us far too often find in short supply.

The techniques I am going to talk about are types of conditioning, programming our conscious and subconscious minds to focus on what we want. But conditioning is nothing new to any of us. Conditioning is no more or less than the stories we tell about ourselves to ourselves. When they are repeated, they become part of us. They have their bases in the stories our parents tell us as little children. My parents told me stories about how I could do anything. They also told me that a lot of other stories, some helpful and some not so much.

There are two principal ways to learn. One is associating new information with a heightened state of awareness – moments, when you exist wholly in the moment, like a runner's high, or in the middle of a car crash when the world seems to slip into slow motion, to impress not just new thoughts but the seeds of new actions. This is the elevated state we are developing. Remember when you made the winning shot in a basketball game, or when you got married or broke your leg or live through some traumatic experience. The same psychological mechanism responsible for PTSD can be harnessed as a powerful tool for impressing ideas upon your brain.

I recognize the experience and I record as much of it as I can in memories so that I can then recreate it. It started in the ski slopes when I started skiing, Skiing is one of my biggest highs. So, every time I was skiing, I was always thinking, I'm out with nature – so wonderful and beautiful. I still love skiing, and I go out there whenever I can.

And then I started implanting ideas in my brain when I was in that peak state. And so, I'd recreate that peak state. At the same time, I'd wire a thought into my brain, or something I wanted to learn. I felt I was experiencing an elevated state and I was learning so much. I felt I was getting in touch with God and so I was, and I wanted to keep recreating that. As it started to take hold, I found a new way that I really enjoyed learning.

Still, I kept coming back to Florida, where there are no ski slopes, and I asked myself "so, how do I recreate this? How do I duplicate this experience?"

So, I found a way to recreate peak states, which you can also learn to do. You do it by changing your physiology by placing yourself mentally in the situation that elevates your mood and your awareness. Holding your focus on that experience, feeling it as much as imagining it consciously, is like a form of self-guided meditation.

The other way to learn is by repetition. You can repeat thoughts and words and intentions continuously and repeatedly for extended periods of time. I've read some incredible stories about people spending their time visualizing happenings that actually haven't yet happened, then making those things happen. This really works. Master this skill and your life is sure to change.

Once you learn how to change your state, you can now learn how to get yourself in a peak state and you can create an important learning opportunity. Because that's one of two ways that actually can take routes. And it doesn't have to come from some re-living any experience.

This is not about changing your personality or making you someone other than who you are. "Be yourself," as Oscar Wilde said, "Everybody else is already taken."

Repetition is the key, but it is not magic. It doesn't matter how often you repeat something if you don't take the action. So long as you're able to take the action, that repeated behavior becomes a habit.

When we make new behaviors, we make new choices and, by making new choices' we're becoming a new person.

Tailor a program to make a lifestyle and a time management system that fits your individual needs and choices as you define your own life course. Keep in mind as you reach each mountain top or plateau that you didn't think you could get to, you'll be able to see a little bit more and as you get to see it a little bit more, to have a little bit more and make a little bit more difference.

Talking specifically about making decisions about your life, whether it's about your thinking, your eating, your exercise plan, when you drink, what you watch, who you hang with. The important constant is committing yourself to the goal of never-ending improvement - but not just improvement. Focused, directed, chosen improvement.

Most people are filled with all kinds of negative thoughts based on subconscious conditioning. What are the negative thoughts?

When we have a belief that we're so anchored to by habitual ways of thinking or by the information that we collect to support our belief, we are not open to as much new information as when we are not anchored to that belief system.

If you've narrow down your belief system to something that just ain't so, it closes the door from the opportunities of what just is. And so, it becomes an obstacle.

I'm going to share with you one of the most important exercises you may ever find to help you create the successful life you seek. You may find that success is something different from what you initially had in mind when you picked up this book. That's fine.

- Create Your Results. Create Your World. Create Your Life
- If wealth, freedom and the power to do and have what you want in life is important to you, this is your opportunity to create them.
- You are not stuck. You already have the unique human ability to imagine and create what does not yet exist.
- All other animals do only what their ancestors and parents did.
- But as a human, you have always had the unique ability to imagine something new and to create it.

- And you have the opportunity now to make that choice... to do what you choose.

This book and your relationship with me is not about believing this material. Belief comes only with experience.

But you can choose what actions you take.

Think of this as a boot camp of the brain, with exercises to make your mind stronger, and to gain access to your full power.

You've always been told to use your mind to create. To reprogram yourself. The secret is, think it and create it.

But up until this moment, nobody may have taught you how.

Step by step, how to program your mind to create what you want.

Here we begin, step by step. With exercises to strengthen you. Strengthen your focus. Strengthen the connection between your mind, body and spirit.

Here we make the unconscious, conscious.

BE AWARE AND NOTICE

WHERE ARE YOU RIGHT NOW?

By picking up the and reading this far, you are choosing to build a new you. That means you have chosen wealth, creativity, well-being, self-fulfillment, and personal power.

You are learning and mastering a step-by-step method which will enhance your inborn ability to create what you choose. You're choosing to fully experience your uniqueness and power, not because this book is powerful, but because you are powerful.

KNOW THIS: REALITY IS CONSTRUCTED BY THE MIND!

Thought is creative and you are the thinker. You're the participator in your life and your life is your results.

Conscious and unconscious negative thoughts produce negative results. Conscious and unconscious positive thoughts produce positive results. You have thousands of thoughts per day and most of them are unconscious. What you think you create as your life.

When you don't take responsibility for your thoughts creating results, you get to be a victim and live other peoples' thoughts and other peoples' lives!

Ultimately, you are totally responsible and therefore POWERFUL whether you choose to exercise your power consciously or not.

WHAT IS THE REAL MEANING OF POWER?

THE ABILITY TO CONSCIOUSLY ACT RESPONSIBLY WE CONSTRUCT OUR OWN RESULTS!

EVERYTHING IN OUR LIFE AND IN OUR WORLD IS BROUGHT INTO OUR AWARENESS THROUGH OUR INDIVIDUAL THOUGHTS. ALL THE THINGS WE OWN, THE RELATIONSHIPS WE ENJOY, THE LOVE AFFAIRS, THE WEALTH AND POWER.

It all begins in your mind – in your thoughts. All of it!

You have always been the creator of your life.

Now it's time to PLAY CONSCIOUSLY! That means we're going to make the unconscious, conscious. This is the first step in gaining mastery.

That means assuming the power to consciously create the results you choose… wealth, love, accomplishment, service. These are choices and they all add up to creating your life through your thoughts. Thoughts are creative and the results you create are your life, conscious or unconscious.

Let's begin to create the new you right now. Take as much time as you need to answer these questions for yourself IN WRITING. It may actually help you to share your answers with someone you love or care about, but then again feel free to keep them totally to yourself.

REPLACING OLD CONDITIONING WITH NEW, CHOSEN CONDITIONING. BECOMING THE PROGRAMMER

You have been conditioned by your habits, your subconscious habits that really rule you. We do not live in a survival environment anymore. But the things that we've been subconsciously conditioned to know are based on the survival model that benefitted our distant ancestors as they stepped out onto the savanna from the relative safety and familiarity of the forest.

For much of our existence on Earth, the kind of cunning caution that you can see every day in the way a house cat explores anything new coming into its environment served humans well. A combination of curiosity and wariness, a readiness to assume that anything new or different could hold a hidden threat, even while needing to examine it further to find out if it did.

This is a basic survival strategy. Unfortunately, it's the opposite of the attitude you need to take into business to achieve your ultimate success.

Instead, you can choose now to take on the mantle of the explorers who, throughout history, took the unknown as a challenge and a means to adventure, as well as potential rewards of fame and riches.

For sure, you'd have to be willing to appear a little crazy in the eyes of more cautious folks, to set off across the vastness of the Pacific Ocean in a long canoe or on a balsa raft, with the hope of coming to a flyspeck of an island in the middle of that endless expanse. Or like Magellan,

Henry the Navigator, or Zheng He, the fourteenth-century Chinese explorer who may have discovered America before Columbus, men who sailed beyond their view of the shoreline, trusting that they could find their way across a featureless plane of water.

Bear in mind as you are deciding how to deal with uncertainty that these explorers became the richest and most celebrated people of their times.

That same devil-may-care attitude has to be a part of the way of thinking you are inculcating in yourself, or you will always be following the herd, looking for reassurance and reinforcement from those around you, and trusting the wisdom of the crowd. That is what most people have done and always will do. And that is precisely why there is room for you at the top if you're willing to make the climb.

As you begin that process, you begin to see all the patterns you have in your life, all the subconscious habits that keep you going around the same circles, over and over, and you begin to pay attention to them. You see places where you can make changes in your life, where you can at least identify thought processes in your life that don't serve you.

Starting with nothing but a burning desire and the decision to take action as your goals, you have already begun your march towards creating it.

I'm old school; the way I do it is with a pen and paper. I date it. I put down what I'm trying to accomplish. I put a target date on it, and I write a statement committing myself to take some action in that direction immediately. And I don't stop until it happens because you haven't failed until you stop trying.

Some people will try to tell you that having a clear vision of your success is all you need to do to realize it. You probably know there's a lot more to it. Stop looking for a lucky break and blaming bad luck for what you haven't accomplished.

A widespread belief is that that success happens to other people; some people are just lucky and some people aren't. That may be true, there's no disputing that sometimes the stars align and sometimes obstacles seem to rise up at every turn. But I think Thomas Jefferson (who was worth listening to on a lot of subjects) was right when he said, "I have always believed in luck, and I've found that the harder I work, the more of it I have."

When it comes to executing a strategy with consistency and the right attitude, luck is what you make of the things life throws at you. The first thing a majority of people need to work on is simply their attitude. Developing the right attitude for success is a skill; it might seem simple, but it's a lifetime endeavor. Consider what thoughts, ideas, and beliefs will support the life you want, which attitude of success are you able to build by directing your thoughts, attitudes, and beliefs? When you do, the remaining pieces of your success plan operate at another level altogether. You have a firm foundation to build on.

Every path has its highs and lows. It becomes a daily discipline to keep your plans and goals in the front of your mind. Everything else in your world will battle for prominence, from the news to your complaining neighbor. You might feel pumped up at the thought of your impending success, but without the right attitude to keep your mind on track, your mood can just as quickly deflate.

Goalsetting is powerful because it helps you learn to focus. You apply it to shape your dreams, to hone in on which actions we need to take to achieve whatever we desire in life. Goals push us to grow and stretch in new directions. In the effort to reach our goals, we become better.

Goals are not merely pipedreams; they need to be specific and ultimately achievable. Nor should you always be shooting for the moon. The journey of a thousand miles begins with a single step. Take your time and give yourself manageable targets to shoot for. Use your successes as a ladder to aim even higher until you have built your stairway to your own personal heaven.

Make sure your goals follow the PRIME Directive. PRIME stands for Precision Resources Immediacy Manageability and Efficacy

- Precision:

Goals must not be vague. Specific goals and milestones to achieving them keep you on track and focused on where you are headed.

- Immediacy:

Your goals should not be something you may hope to accomplish "one day;" they should be the signposts pointing you forward with a clear direction every day.

- Manageability:

One of the most self-destructive mistakes people make is setting themselves up for failure by aiming for goals that are so high that they are unreachable. Reaching for the unreachable star may have been a goal for Don Quixote, but there is a reason his name became the root of "quixotic," meaning a hopeless quest. Sticking to manageable goals makes it far easier to keep going, so you're confident and prepared when you do have to battle windmills.

- Efficacy:

This is a reminder that having achievable and specific plans are only helpful if you are putting them into action. That also means, being willing to make a tactical retreat to reconsider your options and, if necessary, make another plan. Some goals that are simply not realistic and some, however good they looked on paper, just don't work the way they're supposed to in the real world. This is not saying you should not believe in yourself and be persistent, but sometimes reality bends to your will, and sometimes it's you who has to bend a little to avoid breaking. Now let's get down to the most important job you will ever undertake:

MY FIVE MOST NEGATIVE THOUGHTS ABOUT MYSELF AND MY CURRENT SITUATION ARE:

1. _____
   _____
   _____

2. _____
   _____
   _____

3. _____
   _____
   _____

4. _____
   _____
   _____

5. _____
   _____
   _____

Take your time, and enjoy this intimate moment with yourself, as you answer these questions about the list you just made…

My most important and significant negative thought right now is…

What is the biggest obstacle holding you back from creating the life you choose?

THE REVERSE OF MY MOST SIGNIFICANT NEGATIVE THOUGHT IS…

Note: By the reverse, I mean the opposite. The antonym. So, if I said I am fat, the reverse is I am just right. If I said I'm weak, the reverse is I am more powerful than I've ever been. So now…

Let's boil all this down into one simple, brief sentence or two - we will create an affirmation you can remember, carry with you on a card or in your smartphone, so it;s with you at all times…

MY NEW THOUGHT OR AFFIRMATION IS:

_____
_____
_____
_____
_____

BUILD THE NEW YOU NOW.

Whatever your goals have been up to now, let's update them. This is who you are TODAY, and who you are choosing to be.

Remember, you are responsible and powerful. Everything in your life is created by you. Let's take an inventory of what you have created…

Take as much time as you need to answer these questions for yourself IN WRITING. It may actually help you to share your answers with someone you love or care about, but then again feel free to keep them totally to yourself.

RESULTS I HAVE CREATED WHICH I VALUE IN MY LIFE.

1. _____

2. _____

3. _____

4. _____

5. _____

6. _____

7. _____

RESULTS I HAVE CREATED WHICH I DO NOT VALUE IN MY LIFE.

1. _____

2. _____

3. _____

4. _____

5. _____

6. _____

7. _____

Now just beside your list of results you don't value, make a list of the opposites.

In these opposites come directly from your unconscious, and they are a list of results you choose.

As you look over your list of opposites, would the choices on this list improve your life?

Is there anything on this list you don't want? If so, change it. Replace it with something you choose to have.

These may not be the only results you want in your life, but they can give you real focus and increase your power by 1000 fold. These may not be the best and smartest results to create, but they are yours and creating them will give you strength and create a momentum that can carry you exactly where you choose to go.

Finally, let's run this list of your chosen objectives or results through the very practical list of goal setting principles above.

THE KEY TO TRANSFORMATION: START THE DAY

Of course, I get disappointed. Disappointments are part of life, but I trade up - I trade expectations for appreciation. Instead of having expectations, I just appreciate everything that happens. Little shifts in attitude and perspective make all the difference in how I experience my life and how well I perform in every area. You'll find this little change in perspective changes your life, just as it does for me and for so many of my students, who have become wealthier, happier and and infinitely more successful .

Getting centered in the morning gives me the leverage to create better possibilities. When I was younger, if people I worked with weren't doing what I wanted - when they would fail to meet my expectations - I would get frustrated and angry. Now, I have a different view on that; I'm not angry. I just have empathy and compassion and I remember to value the relationship we've built. I hopethey learn from their mistakes, just as I've had to. I am intent on paying attention to everything. When we pay attention to everything, that brings us into the present moment, and, the present moment is where everything happens. All possibilities exist.

That may sound a little bit out there, so bring it down to just starting a meditation practice, evenif only for five minutes a day. Here are a number of YouTube and other sites where you can find guided five-minute meditations to start your morning. The internet is vast and these are just a tiny smattering of what you can find with a search engine primed for "5-minute guided meditations."

- https://www.youtube.com/watch?v=OCorElLKFQE
- https://www.youtube.com/watch?v=nmFUDkj1Aq0
- https://www.youtube.com/watch?v=i50ZAs7v9es
- https://www.youtube.com/watch?v=dEzbdLn2bJc
- https://5minutemeditation.com

It is really important to take some quiet time in life, to become consciously aware of your thought processes, to quiet the mind down so you can get to a place where you're in the present moment and open your mind to the possibilities, where you're in the headspace I like to call the gap. The gap is between your mind's constant churning and the place where the possibilities are. That's the mental space where everything happens. I personally believe there is even a connection there into the quantum world, where thought and physical reality converge. But you needn't be bothered by any of that at the moment, because it makes no difference to what you will do.

The point actually is that to be aware of your thoughts, you have to be in the present moment. The morning practice launches my day, I call the talking part – prayer. The meditating is the listening part.

But what are we asking for in the prayer? I can tell you what I'm seeking. I'm asking for another day to be connected. I'm asking to be led and helped to do what I've willed for myself. That is a good place to start.

The meditation part of my life is the listening to God, which is way more significant in my life now than asking, because I know God's got my back and I can just let him lead me. That's the faith part of it. I don't have to ask specifically anymore. And that's proved to be the difference in my life.

In the past twenty years, I've earned millions of dollars, and achieved what many would evecall important success. On the surface, observers would say the money, the security, and the ability to make a difference in the world came from real estate.

What I'm sharing with you here is the crucial truth that real estate and business experience are valuable tools, but my connection to God, and how I've learned to live my life are the keys to most everything I have and everything I've been able to accomplish and share with the world. Sharing the techniques in this chapter are my unique gift to you that you won't find in business manuals or real estate how-to books.

I've watched so many people's lives change and watched so many of them become successful by learning and developing a routine to START EVERY DAY.

I spend an hour every day between prayer and meditation. That is my baseline to start my day. The other part, getting my body primed and ready comes in the next hour of the day. There's always some exercise and mental preparation, Because when we're talking about our health, we're talking mind, body and spirit - physical, mental, emotional and spiritual health.

Then, for me, there's a daily reading, something I can read in the morning to give my brain some positive input at the start of the day.

I totally believe getting on a daily routine as I have described will be a turning point, not only in your finances but throughout your life, This will make all the difference in your relationships in and outside of work.

By training your subconscious with the right messages, you become so comfortable with them yourself that your communication with others becomes automatically, effortlessly effective. Ridding yourself of any negative programming that may be holding you back changes the way you communicate and the way everyone around you, from customers to your friends and family, perceives you.

Begin to train your subconscious to line up with your conscious so you can create the life of your dreams. Your conscious thinking and your intellectual knowledge will not be enough to carry you to that place that you want to go, until you start retraining the tapes that you've been carrying around all your life. If you can commit to yourself to adopt and perfect through consistent practice, one or two habits a month you will quickly have a completely different life. Even if you successfully adopt two new habits a year, after five years, you'll have ten new habits, and your life will look totally different.

When we change the things that we think about, we behave differently, se feel differently, people respond to us differently, and everything changes for us. Making major life changes feels difficult. What I'm teaching you here doesn't take a huge herculean effort. It just takes commitment and focus. The changes in your life become almost automatic.

You've made a conscious decision that you want to change the way that you're thinking and the way you live, or you wouldn't be reading this book.

Just a few pages ago, we did an exercise that can be the beginning of the stransformation you are seeking.

The list of results you have chosen is a terrific place to start. Those choices come directly from your unconscious.

This moment - is your opportunity to become the person you wish you were!

Focus consciously on one of the results you chose. Make it a habit for a month. Your unconscious mind will keep all the other chosen results in mind with no conscious effot by you.

Take one of these habits and make it part of you this month, then perfect a new one next month. This is going to work for you, and you're going to start to change. You will feel different, you will be different and your life will be different.

Make the decision to start. When's the time to start? It's always right now. When you learn something or hear something that you want to implement in your life, if you don't do it in the first twenty-four hours, most of the time it's gone.

If you're reading this and it's resonating with you, look in the mirror, and look yourself in the eye.

Take your pen and paper out right now. Based on the list of results you've chosen, write down exactly what you are going to do. How you are going to make the result you choose first, part of your life. This has to start right now. You're going to take some kind of action or this opportunity will be gone by the time you flip to the next page. The beginning of the transformation you are committing to will never be more available to you than it is right at this moment. Sieze this opportunity.

When you put your feet on the ground in the morning, you launch your day, and you launch your life. All you have to do now, is put enough days together.

This new person you are becoming is a direct result of the fact that you've consciously directed your thoughts, your actions, and have a focus on the future. You are developing a great sense of where you want to go, you are adding to your strength, your skill and your commitment everyday. Your power and your fulfillment is accumulating. When you have done this enough days in a row, you can't help but make the life that you've been visualizing. You will begin to own the belief in yourself and your God, that will sustain you and build the life you want. You will own that life forever.

Find that power that's greater than yourself, whether you call it Allah, Buddha, Jesus, God, It, creative energy source, creative intelligence. Find that passion inside of yourself. It is calling you, and you will find it easier and easier to hear it, respond to it, and become part of it. A better way to say it, is it becomes a part of you. Soon it will automatically translate into concrete action and change your life.

We each have something inside of us that has been given to us as a special gift. It is waiting to come out, and it wants you as much as you want it. Don't let yourself become so scared to move in the direction of your dreams that your power is diminished. Fear can paralyze if you let it. I'm telling you what you already know in your heart.

You were born with the power to do what you choose in every part of your life. Your upbringing may have robbed you of the confidence and knowledge of yourself and your ability to access that power. You are now making the conscious choice to reacquire that power.

Yes, you are powerful. Rejoice in your power. Share the experience with your God.

You always have been this powerful, so don't get fearful about it. Enjoy your power. Have fun with it. Don't let the power scare you.

Don't make the mistake of confusing seriousness with effectiveness. They are not the same.

Just because you are being invited to create the life you choose, you don't have to become fearful, even if you've had that reaction in the past. There is no point in creating the results you choose if you don't enjoy them.

Get passionate and don't let dream-stealers steal your dreams.

A dream-stealer is somebody who is either afraid they're going to lose you as a friend or somebody who doesn't believe enough in themselves - somebody who's going to tell you shouldn't do something because they can't do it and they don't. A dream stealer can only get in your way, and steal your passion, if you let them You don't need everyone to share your belief.

I have found that I only need myself and God to build a life of wealth, success, fulfillment and a life of serving others. You will find the same. Just stay committed and don't let ancient fears stop you. This will become easier and easier as you build your confidence. But you have to start somewhere and sometime. I pick here and now!

How my life changed after I learned how to start each day

The habit of daily preparation is a building block for the kind of determination and confidence you need to carry you forward through the day. Confidence comes from the discipline to spend that time in an organized, focused manner. Moving your body in the direction that your brain tells you is right for you. When you have confidence that comes from being disciplined for a long period of time and riding the ups and downs, whether you are just getting into shape or starting a new routine.

I've had my morning rituals for over twenty years. They're the backbone of my life. What you might call my morning Launch Today program has been a system of what I formulated after all these years, to put together and to bring it to the world.

I've taught it to enough people already and seen it work for them. I think of it as an implant. Two decades ago, I started and built the habit of exercising in the morning, connecting with my higher power, and writing a journal.

Here is how I've learned to do my Launch Today:

The prayer and meditation part help me begin the day in a creative state of mind, with positive expectation. Then I go to my gym and work out, which is the other part of the equation. Exercising while listening to the stuff I want to learn on headphones. I elevate my mood, jump up my adrenaline and spur me to a peak state, then implant information I can use. I learn something useful every morning, and this has become something I rally look forward to every day.

I've found an effective and almost automatic learning system and I've used it to change my life. It's been a real eye-opener for me.

Every day for the first five years, I literally wrote a letter to God. That's how I built my relationship with God. I did not know how to do it. I knew He was therefrom an early age when He healed me. I continue to write to God, I just don't do it everyday at this stage of my life.

I didn't know how to get closer to God, I just knew I wanted to very much. So, I began a practice of writing to him every day for five years - every day, first thing in the morning.

For me it has been about building that relationship, connecting with that relationship and doing the best I can to be the person God intended me to be, and that I'm supposed to be in this world

I sometimes wrote, "Good morning God and Jesus," and I would thank them for all the blessings that are packed in my life including the ones that I don't see. I would ask God to guide me and point me in the direction of his will for my life today. For a guy who likes to think that I have some control over life, I used to believe I was directing everything. Now it's a little bit more freestyle, because I trust that I couldn't have a roadmap better than the one God has for me, so I don't have to be so rigid. I used to feel I had to know what I was doing every minute.

Of course, I didn't know what I was doing all the time, and what a relief it is, not to be expending energy to support that illusion.

Now, my time with God is more about listening.

I think of it this way. When you get into a room with people who have all the information that you want to know, if you're smart, you keep your mouth shut. That's what's happened with me and God. At one time, I was really needy, so I was reaching for God and asking him what was going on, even though I really already knew.

It's automatic now that I wake up and take a cold shower. This is an important part of my daily routine, because it immediately changes my entire set of feeling, suddenly and all at once. I become a new person, instantly.

Automatically, when I wake up, I say good morning universe. It's automatic that I'm going to go to the gym and listen to whatever recorded material I have selected for the day; it's automatic that I'm going to do a gratitude practice.

I've chosen and developed these habits and they've become automatic. They have helped bring me power and an ability to master every challenge. In fact, as I'm writing this I realize that what used to feel like challenges are now welcome opportunities in my life.

Develop this attitude in your life, and you'll be on your way to the material and spiritual success you are seeking and that you were hoping to find when you selected my book.

The most important part of this is the automatic raising of my self-esteem.

Let me be completely clear. People can accomplish much in life, and be successful in without tapping into that source, without acknowledging it, without even having it. The techniques and methods I am sharing with you are not a requirement to be a or success in real estate or in any other particular business.

I am telling you the way I know to reach your dreams, because it's the way I did it, twice. I've also worked for many years now to study and record how I've been able to do what I have done, to distill it down, as much as possible, to a science, or a set of steps that others can follow to achieve their own success.

There are many people who've accomplished quite a bit and made a difference in the world who have followed other paths. So, you don't have to necessarily do things my way, to tap into the energy generated by your own mind.

I can promise you, though, if you do, you are sending the signal that goes out to the universe. It will magnify and fortify your intentions, and it help you get to where you're going much faster and almost effortlessly. I can promise you that, because I've shared this knowledge with many people already, and I've seen the huge impact it has had on their lives. They achieve spiritual fulfillment, but they also achieve the material success and power they crave, and it comes to them almost automatically.

Having a connection with creative source or God or Jesus or Mohammad or Buddha or your own self - whatever you want to call it - is like adding oil to a machine or gasoline to a car. You can run a car down the road that doesn't have all the parts working and doesn't have the right gasoline and it can still get you somewhere. I'm sharing with you a foolproof way to get where you wish to go with grace, dignity, and community and a feeling. You can and will make a difference. You will get to where you want to go faster, more effortlessly and an empire could spring up around you, if you continue these habits faithfully. I've seen it happen to many people I love, and watching it happen, knowing I am playing a part in their growth, success and mastery feels great. In fact, this is really almost the only thing I really care about at this point, having the financial security, the influence and the independence I craved for much of my life. I've accomplished much of what I set out to do, and I am committed now to helping you do the same.

I am creating the conditions to allow this book to be only the beginning of our lives together – yours and mine.

My passion has always been to make as big a difference in the world as I possibly could. And it's directed and conscious, passionate and persistent. Yet, as consistent as I am, it still took me all this time to finally break out and do this.

You can get a lot more from real estate than I did, if you study real estate as much as I studied human nature, how to change, and how people develop. If you spend all your time in real estate and learn and master how to consciously direct energy, you can make a lot more money than I ever did in real estate. And, many people would call me rich.

Just the same, you can apply this formula and start feeling better about yourself as you move in the direction of what you believe you can do.

Magical things will start to happen in your life. The feel magical, but this is really not magic, it's actually activity breeding productivity. You make a decision, you take action, you believe in yourself, you trust in the process, you trust in the higher power, you trust in your calling. And you start to see things happen.

Keep in mind that negative things happen quicker than positive things. This is not yet another appeal to luck. The results of negative actions can often show up almost overnight. Catastrophes almost always happen suddenly. In fact, if you had the time to prepare, for the challenge, it wouldn't be a catastrophe. Say, you drank really hard last night and you have a hangover. That is an example of a negative activity having immediate results.

Positive results can and usually will take time. The seeds that you plant, like the farmer plant seeds, will reap positive results in your life, if they are allowed some time to take root. The results of positive actions take time and concerted effort.

When you start your own Launch Today rituals in the morning, it could be a couple of days or even a couple of weeks before you start to feel some impetus or positive energy in your life. It may not happen overnight. I *can* almost guarantee if you implement a gratitude practice every day, recognizing the things you have to be grateful for, at some point within the 90 days, you will begin to find something that you haven't experienced before.

Once more: here is your new morning ritual. After you get started, and learn the ropes, you can feel free to make modifications to make this yours, but this is as good a place as any to start.

1. Wake up in the morning and say, "Good morning God or Universe – however you experience this incomprehensible power that is greater than us.

2. Immediately jump into a COLD shower. This jerks you into the present, and immediately changes you into a new you. You are here for transformation, and this is an important secret to make it easier. You don't have to struggle with the past. As I said, you have the experience of being jerked into the moment, which is exactly where you want to be.

3. Meditate for just a few minutes, or as long as you like. I've given you some links to guided meditations. Find your own, record your own. Own this process.

4. Sit in peace and connect to your God – however you experience him or whatever you choose to call him or it. I found for several years, that writing a letter to God was a great way for me to get my thoughts and desires in order and to connect to God. After a while, I even had him write back to me.

5. Do some kind of rigorous exercise. I love to go to the gym every morning and do a strenuous work out, while listening to a recording of something I've chosen to learn and master. A long walk or run also works well for many people. The point is to change your body, generate endorphins in your brain, and become that powerful, energetic person you crave to be.

Follow this routine every day. After a very short while, it will become a habit, and it will become an important part of you. This will make everything else you do, and everything we do and learn together,

Many people, who started out with me as trainees or students, tell me the professional training in real estate and business is useful and valuable, but there are many places to get it. The indispensable part is this lesson in the habits of mastering life.

HOW YOU LIVE YOUR LIFE

You must teach yourself to operate from a place of confidence and a belief that there's something working within you on a daily basis.

I don't try. I'm not trying. I'm doing it. My point is, we don't use words like try and can't and possible, and maybe. We don't have any doubt. When we take control, consciously, of the way that we think, we can actually take control of life and consciously direct much of what happens.

A new form of self-confidence can be yours, when you reach the place where you know that whatever you decide to do, will get done. You will follow through and you will succeed. Just this knowledge is where the confidence comes from, not from the belief that accomplishments will come easy.

This confidence comes from the knowledge that you are relentless, and that you will never give up until you've achieved your objective.

Another, higher level of confidence would be based on faith - unshakable faith - that you are connected to the source, and that you're working with him

The best way to enhance your self-esteem is to identify what your priorities are in five or six key areas of your life. And be specific.

For me, Number One would be God. You may call it what you want, creative intelligence, or any of those names – however you describe that incomprehensible collective consciousness that we know is there, even though we can't define it.

Number Two for me is health.

Number Three is family;

Four is finances will;

Five would be my contributions to the world;

And Number Six would probably be fun. And under each one of those priorities, there are categories of activities that I serve to implement them.

The key point right now is to get started. Take that first step. Make some goals for yourself. Decide what your priorities are. Take some action each day in the direction of what those may be, and create the life of your dreams. That chosen life is waiting for you. As a matter of fact, it's calling you.

Become a doer. Make this life something magnificent. The life is yours to live.

Take action now: one day, one step, one person at a time.

I think everybody now knows, thanks to modern science, that our thoughts can make us sick. The other side of that coin is our thoughts can make us well. And if those two things are true, which they are, that has significant implications about how we can direct our life. Thoughts are energy and the way we think will actually determine our life. But if we haven't really mastered this idea, and learned to use it, it's unlikely that we're going to start to pay attention to what we're thinking.

When you make specific, goal directed, deliberate, disciplined action in the direction of your chosen results, change repeatedly comes to you over weeks, months, and years. You develop the self-discipline that gives you the confidence that you're becoming the person you're intended to be. It comes down to self-discipline in all the areas of your life.

The subconscious conditioning that influences, and even rules the daily behavior of most of humanity is inherited from a distant past. It's strong, but it can be surmounted by reconditioning yourself. Once you know the trick of practicing a new response, repeating it and making it part of your life, confident that as it becomes a habit and becomes part of your unconscious, it can replace those anachronistic, limiting responses and behaviors. You are free, and able to respond – in the present – as you consciously choose.

This is simply a story of taking responsibility. Once you know your responses are choices, and that you can program yourself any way you choose, you are free.

Responsibility means knowing you are the power in your life, and that everything you create is your responsibility – you are becoming master of your own destiny. You are no longer a supporting actor in someone else's life. You are choosing. Responsibility equals power!

This is the secret of real mastery, and you will be exploring and pushing out your limits for years.

So, if you've lined up your subconscious with who you are right now and your vision of the future, your subconscious motivations and behaviors are no longer dictated by the fears and memories of the past. Then, all of a sudden, there's no default to anything. You have the discipline to regularly decide, "Today I'm going to wake up and be the best expression of myself, AND HERE IS WHAT THAT LOOKS LIKE!"

Step one is getting started on any of your priorities. Mine was God. So, Step One was making a connection.

Step two was to build my relationship with my God.

As you build real confidence, believe in your ability and courage to persevere and get through the obstacles and disappointments. The magic is those obstacles cease to bother you very much.

You've got to get through bad breaks. You've got to get through the market crashing. You've got to get through people leaving, through sickness. You just get through life and keep on progressing, but with real confidence – not that everything will work right, not that every objective will come to you easily, but that you will prevail in the end. You don't have to believe you are the best player, you just have to know you will never give up, and will always be back until you have prevailed. Until you have accomplished what you set out to do.

As Bjorn Borg, the great tennis champion said, all I have to do is get the last ball over the net.

Practice directing your thinking. Practice concentrating. No matter what goals you set, it is only your level of commitment that counts. In every endeavor and walk of life, the skill will come with practice.

Whatever you decide to master, whether it's writing and publishing books, or building a real estate empire. When your goal is clearly articulated and becomes increasingly important to you as your confidence grows, you'll feel yourself becoming more resourceful. You'll feel your passion growing and even becoming obsession. You learn to be present, and in the moment. You receive and attract, instead of hunting.

Keeping yourself open to new ideas and ready to accept and make the best of the unexpected is even more essential, as you become more adept at self-programming.

Everybody has the same opportunity to make choices that will empower them. We all have access to information enough to get in great physical shape, to build a fulfilling spiritual life, to lots of money and to serve.

What you are learning here took me a lifetime to understand, and this way of living – the mental and spiritual game - is the secret to creating. I can tell you for sure, that people with this kind of confidence, discipline and commitment are able to out-play and to succeed and surpass people with more talent, who start with greater resources, but without this understanding of mastery, perseverance, and developed inner strength. This is where your relationship with God becomes crucial.

You are learning and becoming confident that you are not playing the game alone. You are an important part of the greatest team on earth – You and God.

Wanting is where it all starts. The big difference in your life comes when you don't only want, but develop the strength and ability to THINK LIKE AN INVESTOR – to follow the lesson I shared with you at the beginning of this book.

In fact, it would be a great idea for you to go back to the beginning right now, now that you've come so far. You are already a different, stronger, more confident, more able, more motivated person than you were when you started reading and studying this book. It seems that was ages ago in a different lifetime, doesn't it?

Everything is available to you, if you know you want it, know what it takes to make the decision to go and get it, then take action every day forever, until you've achieved your objective.

Every day will be like you are a kid in a candy store on Christmas. Your heart will open. You will find the passion to fulfill your destiny.

Amazingly, my students tell me they experience the same thing I did as I was reaching my material goals. They say they're shocked by how easy it was to accomplish amazing things, once they gained the confidence, commitment and the skill to execute in real estate, and in any area of endeavor.

Constant never-ending improvement is the key to a happy life because when you have your priorities in order, you take baby steps in the direction of where you going, and you take them consistently. No one can stop you.

Crawl before you walk, walk before you run, run before you sprint. Sprint, before you take off and you will build a life of magnificence.

It will be magic. You'll build a skyscraper. You'll be brimming with the pride of accomplishment, but you'll always give credit to your team and to your God.

You will make a difference. You'll be fulfilled. You'll find happiness and you'll be rich beyond your wildest dreams, because when we're talking about riches, you'll remember how it all started with that positive mental attitude. Whatever the negative side, whether it's jealousy, greed, ego, whatever it is that's negative, you will find a way to replace it with the opposite, positive thought, and you'll find all the help you need along the way.

Start paying attention to your thinking process and that will become vital in success in your life. You remember the childhood taunt, "Sticks and stones can break your bones, but words will never hurt you."

It's not true. Bones and things that break can heal: words penetrate you; the words that damage us the most, are the ones that we tell ourselves.

The more you take responsibility for your self-talk, the more you ware clear on the language you choose to use, the stronger and more accomplished you will feel yourself becoming. The more practiced and the more confident you become with this process, the easier it is for you to continue. You make decisions and you take action. If you want progress and success, you've got to stop trying. Try just isn't good enough. If you really want something, there's no such thing as try. You just keep going until you get what you're going for. That takes persistence and a burning desire after you've made a decision to take action in the direction of what you want to have in your life, all things are possible. Nothing's impossible.

Again, let's review the words to avoid and to remove from your life, because they do nothing to move you toward success you are committed to achieve. They are:

Try - we don't try, we accomplish and succeed.

Problem – we don't face problems, we rise to challenges

Can't – we can

The strength you get from taking control of your life.

We are in agreement here that the habits that we have in our life determine the quality of our lives. When we successfully choose our behaviors, then make our chosen behavior into habits through commitment and repetition, we're in fact consciously changing our lives. And once those behaviors we've chosen become habits and part of our unconscious, the results we've chosen feel as though they are being accomplished effortlessly.

Each one of us individually has a certain comfort zone. When we leave it we encounter resistance from ourselves, just as when we try to move others out of their comfort zones, they often resist, even if what we are suggesting is likely to make an important improvement in their lives. The bottom line is, we often value comfort – avoiding change – over positive results.

Also, when you move outside your normal zone, you may encounter resistance from your friends and family. Generally, they're comfortable with the old you that they are accustomed to, and also have a tendency to project their doubts and insecurities about themselves on to you. Be prepared for this, and hopefully you can help them reconcile themselves to the new you.

I've often seen situations where they just can't. Your job is to make sure you surround yourself with people who support your new objectives, and contribute to them. When the people who you have grown to love begin to hold you back, you have a crucial decision to make.

Might as well think this through right now. How committee are you? How much do you want the success you seek, and what are you willing to pay or give up in order to achieve it?

I wish for the best for everyone, but I also know that part of my edge, and part of what has helped me achieve what many would call great financial and career success, has been my ability to trust God, deal with uncertainty, Transend fear, and treat obstacles as challenges and opportunities.

I am committed to helping as many people as possible to find the best in themselves, however I can't help appreciating the fact that the competition would be much stiffer if everyone was a great player.

I'm one of those people who, when you tell me I can't do something, I'm going to do it. That's going to inspire me to make sure that I do more of it. I route for everyone's success, and also, I know there is a lot of room at the top, because most people are afraid to compete at that level.

I've met a lot of people who never did find the wherewithal to pursue their grandest dreams, and many have regretted it deeply. Those are the souls who stand on the precipice, looking out at the vast horizon stretched in front of them, yet remain paralyzed by fear, and are unable to get themselves to make the big move into opportunity. They see the unknown as danger, when you and I see it as adventure and opportunity

You don't have to follow that path. Instead, you can choose a brighter way. In order to set your sights on the heights you hope to reach, first you need to identify what success means for you.

Take a few minutes right now, and lets commit to writing a study of the values and ideas that are most important to you.

What do you truly value in your life?

What are the goals and objectives for which you are willing to sacrifice?

What are you willing to sacrifice? How far are you willing to go in your quest for your new life?

Who and what do you really love?

What are the little and big factors that make life worthwhile?

How have your values changed while you've been reading this book and working on creating your new life?

_____

_____

_____

_____

_____

By answering these questions, you define success for yourself. Be as specific as you can considering the elements that go into forming the life you'd like to lead.

Your attitude is the result of thoughts. Thoughts are simply electrical impulses charting a pathway through your cerebral cortex. The more times the nerve cells fire in a particular order and stimulate the same cells down the line, in turn, the easier time the signal has of propagating the same way in the future. The habits of mind that fill your thoughts with images of success or stories of failure are literally paths that have been formed by repetition.

They feel fixed, but they were created by repetition and they can be changed exactly the same way.

From this moment forth, you must make a decision, to remain aware of what you are thinking at all times.

Are the thoughts that seep into your consciousness consistent with your chosen goals and objectives? If not, simply change them. Make the decision, write down the old thought, cross it out, and replace it with the new thought you choose.

Sure, things happen in life you can't control. You cannot control all the circumstances in which you find yourself, but you can change yourself, and you can choose your thoughts. The more you practice this the better you will get at it. You have full authority to do that.

The right attitude treats every failure as an invitation to try and do better, and a lesson in what didn't work and why. It is redefined now, in your life as an opportunity for correction.

Once you've begun to master the art of looking at things with a new perspective, things don't just start going your way – not immediately and not certainly. Every road has highs and lows. Sometimes, your greatest challenge is maintaining that positive attitude. It's a daily discipline to remain mindful and determined in the face of adversity.

The world can be an attention-suck and a distraction. But without the right attitude to keep your mindset on track, your plan is likely to fail.

Please know, this is not a fad. Wild enthusiasm is not the same as determined, focused confidence. One can lead to brash, ill-conceived decisions, which may, in turn, lead to disastrous consequences. The other is bold, stepwise progress with the agility to bend to new circumstances. Which do you think ends to give better results?

One of the tremendous gifts of our human intellect is the power to have dreams of a better life and the imagination and ingenuity to picture a way to live out those dreams. We not only can but almost instinctively do dream of a better situation for ourselves and our families. We have been doing it for a couple of million years, since the first "caveman" (to borrow an archaic term) chipped away at a piece of slate until it had a sharp point on one end, while the other fit neatly into his palm – making a hand ax, the first true stone tool.

Nowadays, we dream of better financial, emotional, healthful lives. We have the ability not only to dream but to follow our dreams with the foresight to strategize about how to achieve those dreams. Have you ever just sat down and thought through your values to decide what you really want? Have you taken the time to have that conversation with your loved ones? Listen quietly to your heart, to see where you live in your dreams. Share them. Everyone has them. They may even sound foolish when you first try to talk about them. But that's just your fears and self-doubt telling you stories.

Having a clear-eyed vision of your goal is a necessary, but not sufficient condition for your achieving all you want in life. You also need to know how to get there. What are the steps that other people have taken to get where you want to be? Can you emulate them, learn from their successes and failures, whether by reading about them or interviewing them first-hand?

Or, if your circumstances and, even more likely, your talents and skill-set do not align with the way they did it, how can you reach the same place by a different route? You need a personal development plan to help direct your energies on a daily, weekly, monthly and long-term basis. And, remember, if you're not following your own plan for your future, you are most likely working as a cog in someone else's dream machine.

Think about what thrills you. Recall what Confucius said about not ever having to work if you love what you do?

What is your ideal occupation? If education and training were not an issue, and if you already had all the money you'd need to satisfy your needs and desires, what would you be doing?

Bear in mind that "sitting on the couch, watching my stories and eating bonbons" is not only a hard job to find, but it gets old, fast. Hardly anyone actually wants to be the idle rich, though it is better than being the idle poor.

So, what would you *love* to be doing? What do you have a driving urge to accomplish? What would you try if you were immune to the fear of failure?

Now, forget all the questions and go for a walk (or a bike ride, or a drive, if you have some bucolic route with no traffic to aggravate you, and no radio). Let your mind wander and your dreams condense and float through your mind like clouds.

Record them as they come to you. (Don't you love smartphones?) Don't edit yourself. Don't reject anything as too far out or too unlikely. This is an exercise in blue-sky thinking. There are no wrong or too over-the-top answers. Sorting them and judging them comes later.

Set aside some time after you've had a chance to let the ideas you recorded settle out. What dreams are most important for you to pursue?

Which are the most viable? Which would you love to do the most? Rank them in the order you intend to achieve them. Remember, the purpose is to always be acting to move closer to reaching your goals, not just dreaming of the day.

The late New York Governor Mario Cuomo once said that politicians "campaign in poetry, but ... govern in prose." Life works much the same way. We dream long-term, but we live day-to-day.

We dream of the future and live in the present. Still, having a long-term vision in your life gives you a roadmap and a direction to point yourself in. In the end, that is all anyone can expect to have. As the old Yiddish proverb has it, a man makes his plans, and God laughs. We count on our long-range goals to help get us to get past the inevitable short-term obstacles we will encounter on the way. The more strongly we are able to focus on our goals are, the more we're capable of acting to ensure they actually come to pass.

Goalsetting is also not some kind of secret that has to be revealed to you and there are no rigorous physical and spiritual exercises you have to master to earn your different colored belts of rank. There is a formula that is not hard to put down in a series of steps and not hard to follow the same way.

Determining with conviction what you hope to achieve in the future begins with an honest assessment of where you stand right now. How satisfied are you with your life as it is today? Not terribly, or you wouldn't still be reading this book. Still, maybe life is good, or good enough. And yet, you do have something, a spark that you keep from going out until you can drop it into some kindling and let it catch and become a blazing hot desire in your core.

Put it down on paper (or pixels – don't forget, I'm old). However, you record it, write, out your present situation and what you envision changing to create your dream life. Make a list and check off each one that meets or exceeds, that you are satisfied with. Why? Simple, until you know where you are, you can't really know where you're going and how far you have to go to get there. It's your baseline, your starting point.

This is also a working document, so maybe it's better to do it on a laptop or phone. Go back to it on a weekly or biweekly basis. As things go on, perhaps you'll need to revisit it less. The point is not just to review where you were some time in the past, though charting your progress can be helpful. Reviewing your goals and plans for reaching them gives you the opportunity to revise and change them. With any luck (read "hard work"), you will be taking steps and passing interim goals, and the farther you go, the more clear you may become about what it is you *really* want.

Once you know what you're looking for you'll begin the forward momentum. Some people go faster, some will go slower, but you have been armed with a roadmap for vibrant health, increased energy, better friendships, deeper relationships, more harmony in your life, a better relationship with themselves, a better relationship with their partners, a very much better relationship with God.

I found that the people that I liked the least, if I had enough time to spend with them, we share a lot more in common than whatever divides us because everybody's really the same, deep down. We may have different characteristics and different personalities, but given enough time with anybody, basically, we're all the same. So, I don't judge; ego means nothing and judgment is unacceptable. Every human being deserves respect, even myself.

I believe without any doubt, there is some creative, intelligent force or source, and everybody has it. Scientists have found what for a time they called the "God particle," a manifestation of a force field that permeates the universe and gives matter the mass that makes it matter. As I see it, you tap into that source, which is God or everything that is, or the energy web. All potentials are there.

One of the great truths in life, one of the things that those of us who are fortunate enough to become wealthy almost inevitably learn (I say almost inevitably because there are some people who just refuse to learn, no matter what field you're in) is that money *really can't* buy happiness. To be sure, I've been rich and poor, both, and I have no doubts – I prefer rich. But there comes a point where having more just ceases to be a big deal. When he was ranked the world's richest man, Bill Gates explained that having more money simply had no real meaning to him. There was already nothing he couldn't afford. And, as he put it, "you can't fly any faster, you can't eat any better."

Sociologists who studied lottery winners, the ultimate example of a lucky soul. They concluded that up to about $75,000 (in 2010 or thereabouts), having more money equated with fewer money worries and greater satisfaction. But once they were beyond where more money meant more security, being able to accumulate more stuff just did not bring commensurate rewards. Just ask Bill Gates. He decided the best way he could use his money to make himself happy was to spend the rest of his life giving it away. Hence, we have the Gates Foundation and the Giving Pledge, convincing other billionaires of the virtue of giving it all away.

For me, there has always been a search for more. At one time, it was more money, more houses and more income coming in. Then, it was more fun, more drugs and partying, finally, after years on that treadmill, it became more connection to God and more connection to the heart.

Everybody thinks the brain is where it's at, but for me, it's from deep in my heart that I send my love into the world.

What is it that we're really looking for? We're looking for love and connection that unify our minds with individuals. For me, that has been about finding God – whatever that means to you. I have a vision very clear and I have a partner, God, that's directing everything. You don't have to find my God. You have to find your own. where I'm at now, I'm finding parallels between these lessons I've learned through a life in real estate and decades now in Recovery with quantum physics, so I'm looking for guys that are talking and teaching and using science as the background for my understanding of how the brain works.

I am endeavoring to be scientific but I am not a scientist and not everything I say will necessarily line up exactly with what one or another theoretical physicist might say. Rather, it is a framework on which I have hung my own interpretations and understanding, and sometimes it drifts across the line between science and philosophy, hard facts and spiritual truth.

I would think that ninety-nine percent of the world's people in some way, shape or form have the same priorities that I have: spirituality, or a relationship with God, the universe or the Higgs boson; my health, family, and friends, third, being financially sound is my fourth priority, and giving back to the world is the fifth, which my fourth priority helps make possible. Last but not least, is fun because if you're not having fun, you're still not doing it right. There have been times in my life when it probably looked like fun was the most important thing and there are times in life. But overall, those are my priorities and my actions have centered around those priorities for much of my life.

There is a source, and I call it God because I'm American and that's the language I know. I believe that source is, I don't know if it's you or somebody else probably it's light because everybody has light. Even if they're living in a place where they don't have a language for it, they know light, which I think of infinite energy or, infinite intelligence. Call it Buddha; call it Allah or Jesus, or just energy; it could be creative intelligence.

I believe that everybody, every human being at some point in their life got a feeling that they knew something was greater than themselves. And that feeling that was also the light in that they saw and connected them to something else was also the light that they're seeking, which will open up the world to unlimited possibilities, their worlds to unlimited possibilities. Every human being has felt at some point is actually the light that we have to find that will bring us towards it and then come towards us because that is actually close to what our burning desire is in God's intention for your life is to begin a process of building a relationship with that higher power.

Each one of us inside of us, a light has been there since we were born. It flickers here and there through Don't get scared. That takes discipline. Most of us, we go back to what we're already comfortable in doing, but when that light in, that desire wakes up at any point in your life, it's up to you to move towards it. When you get that flicker, go towards it.

The three best decisions I ever made were to stop using drugs and alcohol, making God a working part of my life, co-creating my life with God, and to understand that real estate is the vehicle that I can utilize to help myself be free, but it's the vehicle that can attract people to me so I can make a difference in other people's lives.

I have is grown into this place where I'm really comfortable just letting God take me, take me where he takes me. Especially on a daily basis, I obviously have to make plans and get on a plane or drive to places. I have a vision for my life and have a business plan at all that when in each moment of each day I can surrender because of that faith that comes from a process of spending time. It's like with people, the more time you spend with them, the more you're going to get to know them. And so, I find myself waking up earlier, earlier every day so I can carve out this special time to build my faith

Now is the doorway to your future and our thoughts are the key to open the door.

For me, success and peace of mind came together when I learned to let myself surrender, and to let God guide me.

THE NEW YOU

The most important and valuable part, so far, of your new journey:

Write a short description of the new you – the person you now choose to become – the person you are becoming right at this moment…

_____

_____

_____

_____

_____

_____

This little story you've written about whom you choose to be, will develop into a solid mental picture if you let it. Keep rereading it, modifying it when you want to, and picturing different aspects of this new you every morning, as you meditate.

If you use a guided meditation, like the examples I listed for you earlier, take a minute or two at the end. Stay quiet and contemplate this new you. Picture it. Allow your image of that new person you choose to be, to grow inside you. Allow it to become more concrete.

You'll find this becomes easier, the more you practice imagining this new you. It will become easier, and your mental picture will become more concrete. As time goes on, this image of the new you that you choose to be, will become the you that you are, in the moment, in real time.

This process will be worth a lot of money to you, if that is what you want, and it will serve as your path to happiness and fulfillment.

Congratulations on your success. You deserve it!

SOME QUANTUM MUSINGS

We've all been taught to lead with our brains, to think things through and try, as best as we are able, to make the logical choice, and to have faith that the logical decision will be the right one. There is, however, another place that we operate from in reality - the level of feelings, emotions, faith and soul, which are centered in the heart. And, we need them both.

When I say that, I mean not just that we should be motivated by compassion and sympathy, or to recite the Golden Rule – not that those are bad ideas in themselves. Rather, that you have no choice. Whether you acknowledge it or not, your choices and decisions, the very ways you frame the questions, reflect your inner-feelings and beliefs. You cannot avoid them. You can only learn to recognize them, to bring them out of the shadows of your mind, so that their influence on you is not hidden below the surface.

Bringing your emotional life and belief system into the open not only makes their influence more apparent. By aligning your thoughts and actions to your beliefs, you can begin to channel the benefits you are gaining, through clarity and constant, never-ending improvement, back out into the universe. The positive energy you put out is real, as well, and it affects you, your life and the lives of the people around you. In my own life, I have strong evidence that my thoughts have everything to do with the kind of people, ideas and opportunities that come to me.

Even if this idea seems foreign to you – it did to me a long time ago, before I proved to myself how well it works – why not try it on for size? See how your life changes when you are the director of your thoughts, and when you choose them knowingly based on the kind of results, and the kind of life you want to create for yourself.

When I started out, I did not have these insights. I was very directed - driven to make a plan and stick to it, no matter what. That is a way forward because, as I've said before, you haven't failed as long as you keep learning from your experiences and continue to press forward. You only fail when you give up.

Thoughts are things, literally. Everything is energy, including the flashes of electricity coursing through the pathways of your brain. The EEG machine traces the broad outlines of those thought patterns. They exist in the real world; thoughts do affect matter. This much is something that pretty much all physicists understand as true, or as close to the truth as science gets.

When physicists talk to nonscientists about matter and energy, they usually talk about the electrons, protons, and neutrons that make up atoms, and the quarks that make up electrons, neutrons and protons as if they are infinitesimal particles, like unimaginably small grains of sand. They describe energy mostly as waves, like electromagnetism. This was actually the science of the 19th and early 20th centuries.

But, among themselves, today's physicists speak of both matter and energy as sometimes behaving in a particle-like way and in a wave-like way at other times. What is more, and far harder to wrap your head around, they can act either way, *depending on how you choose to measure it.*

This actually isn't some metaphysical belief I have. Since it works, that would be enough for me, but amazingly, these ideas, which were developed as metaphors thousands of years ago, are now actually being proven in laboratories around the world!

Do an experiment looking for wave interference, that's what you get; look for particles, and there they are. The truly spooky part is that if you try to measure both the waves and the particles at once, you get an average of the two, half acting wave-like and half particle-like. In other words, the physical results are affected by the way they are observed. Scientists are now proving what wise men have always known. Thoughts create and change reality, so intention creates results.

People have been showing as much in experiments for at least 150 years. For the last 100 or so, the explanation most scientists are taught to rely on to explain the seemingly contradictory "double-slit experiment" is called the Heisenberg Uncertainty Principle. Google it. It's much too complicated to get into here, but in part, it says that whether the experiment is set up to find light or electricity acting like waves or particles depends on how you set up the experiment.

One of the conclusions you can draw from this is that what you believe to be true can become true, as long as you keep impressing that thought on your mind and acting on it. Shockingly, physics is catching up with metaphysics.

As far out as some of what I have begun to learn about this may appear, bear in mind that it is grounded in actual science. On the other hand, I am not a scientist and I lay no claim to being an expert in these things. You are here, because I've created financial, social and life results that many want to duplicate. I'm just sharing with you how I learned to do it.

Just like everything else in this book, this section is based upon my experience, and it's the closest thing to the truth, as I have been able to understand it. A lot of it is my interpretation of how things feel that have come to me. They come from the direction of feelings, straight from, or straight into my heart, and my mind is following behind, trying to make sense of these bursts of understanding that energy is everything.

Thoughts are the language of the mind, and feelings are the language of the body. When you're finally capable of synching up your thoughts and feelings, it opens your heart and sends a signal to the brain. That signal is love in action. I'm beginning to think that unity between the heart and the brain is even more powerful than thinking, even as thinking has to remain a part of it.

It's important to understand that none of this comes without work and dedication; it takes time. Somebody who has achieved something or gotten somewhere that you haven't yet, may have been at it longer, or focused their thoughts and energy, and you still have to impress what you are creating on the energy web long enough to have it manifest.

God is the easiest way for me to talk about this all-pervasive presence, the consciousness at the heart of the universe. Still, some of what I am talking about could be a new discovery (actually, it was predicted decades ago, but only proven in the lab recently) physicists call the Higgs Field, an energy field spread evenly across every region of the universe.

A fundamental particle known as the Higgs boson (remember, sometimes a wave, sometimes a particle, depending) allows the field to continuously interact with other particles, such as the electron. Elementary particles, and thus everything from this book to the air we breathe and the stars themselves, have mass because they are interacting with the field. Think of it as like a ball rolling through a pool of molasses, slowing down as it moves along. I am not sure if the Higgs field is what I am calling the "energy web," but that seems right to me.

The bottom line is, whether you take this as a metaphor for reality, or you embrace it all as your physical reality, learning to work within it, to be a part of it, to connect to it, and to be very intentional about how you think and what you feed into and receive from the world, is the secret of producing the life you want. If the life you want is material wealth, financial and emotional freedom, power, happiness, and love, I am sharing with you, as a mentor who has been able to attain some of what you want for yourself, that these ideas – learning to be part of the universal mind – is as important to your results as the regular business skills and knowledge you get in every self-help and how-to book on real estate, business, relationships and life.

When you can impress a thought upon the energy web and hold on to it for long enough, when it is activated by a burning desire, and implemented with a strategic plan, with a never-give-up commitment to making it happen, I have learned that it's inevitable that you can make *anything* happen. Certainly, you can make a fortune in real estate, if that's where you want to focus your energy.

Everything vibrates at a different frequency. The desk, the chair, the phone, everything is made up of neurons, protons – subatomic particles. As scientist develop better tools, they keep finding smaller and more basic ones. They keep trying to split them, and they keep finding more, seemingly to infinity. There's a whole lot in the space between me and a computer, or me and the wall, we just don't see it. It's vibrating at different frequencies, and we're all part of that energy web.

Everything out there is available to every single person. Every thought that's ever been had is still vibrating through the universe, whether we can tune into them or not. All the information is available. It is what we're made of - congealed bits of spinning energy, all vibrating at a coherent frequency. So, the energy that we produce with our thoughts and the vibrations they put out are that same thing, but not yet turned into matter but part of that web. The web is something that connects us and everything together; we don't see it, but it's there.

It appears that our thought, held continuously and impressed upon the energy web that's out there, can be made manifest. I know in the real estate world, and in the mind over matter world - in any world - if you can find somebody who can show you a path or lead you to the water so you can drink it, that is a much faster path to get there than to try to explore every single thing and think you have to create everything for yourself. Everything's connected. Everything's in the energy web. Our minds are connected. Our thinking is the language of our brain that sends a signal into the web.

As we raise our consciousness, we attract more like-minded things because our brain sends the signal out. We send a signal into the web and our feeling is the magnet. It brings back to us the energy that resonates and vibrates with us. The energy of the web is real; we're all part of it. And we direct energy, consciously or unconsciously.

When I had nothing, I was just exercising and meditating and praying and reading. Now, I'm trying to help people, one person at a time, one community, and by that, I mean a real estate community, a recovery community could mean a corporate community. We impress our thinking and our thought process upon a person and, if that person leads us to a bigger circle upon that community, then we unify the people with a thinking process and a common shared vision that life can be better together. At the beginning of trying to build something that can radically transform people, of necessity, it was a process of helping one person, then helping another person because that was all the reach I had at the time.

Now I hope what I am building is going to be able to help more people, building a bigger skyscraper with a broader reach and greater possibilities for impressing our dreams onto the energy web and actualizing it in the real world through our actions.

As we learn more, we're bringing the information to the people and teaching ways people can leverage who they are and get into action so they can become something different – become more. Working with one another, helping elevate our minds, our thoughts and our businesses, you take one person to one community, to one city or one state, and bring that model out into the world.

Once we realize we're all part of the energy web, we understand that what we do here affects somebody on the other side of the world, and that they are also part of us. I'm getting a sense that we're all connected and that even the bugs or the ants are all part of it. I don't know how this exactly happened for me, but I'm having a hard time killing bugs now even though there's a bee or a roach in my house.

What I hope to be doing here is unifying the minds of human beings to connect on a higher vibrational frequency, so together, we can have an impact on the energy web to create lasting peace and happiness in the world. I have a bigger foundation to work from now, in terms of both financial and social resources but also, I hope, in growing wisdom, as well.

I think most people dream about peace, joy, happiness, unity, love, compassion, empathy, oneness. It's happening one person, one community, one state at a time, the same as when I was building a business or building a network marketing team. I have no doubt that we're on track and moving forward. It's happening everywhere in small little pieces and large, with like-minded people. I think I'm getting closer and closer to the people that are having a bigger influence on the world in this arena.

I was always the kind to direct things, but I was uncertain about everything and how it would work out. Now, I go forward not planning every step and not trying to control every aspect of the future, certain that God is leading every step. At this stage in my life, I don't see the necessity in making lots of plans and I just go with the flow. And so, I follow the path laid at my feet in certainty with uncertainty.

The God that I know and the faith that I have in him is actually working through us right now to unify the world because conflict separates the world and we need to love it. A connection is what everybody's really looking for above and beyond the dogmas attached to religions across the world. The heart is going to be the beat that pulses - that spreads energies throughout the world.

I can see that we're just energy that has come to farm, and we're made in the image and likeness of God. Then, sometimes I think, in the way that a Hindu Yogi or a Buddhist Bodhisattva might put it, I am God. I keep my head from growing too large, by my thoughts when I look at my wife. I also think she's God, too. You're God too, because I think we're all God. I'm energy. I'm made in the image and likeness of God. He's not separate. We're part of Him but He is bigger. It's like I'm a person and my arm is my arm, but my arm is not me.

Of course, you can take all of that with a grain of salt, if you wish. I firmly believe that the approach and methods I've outlined in this book can lead to a life of total fulfillment, as it has for me. If what you take from it is a how-to guide to building a real estate empire that can secure your family's financial wellbeing for the foreseeable future and nothing more, that is all well and good, too. As I have said before, fulfillment is personal, and everyone views it through a different lens.

This is not the only guidebook, or the only pathway to success; it is my path – one I am confident will work for you if you work with it. I'm sure because I've used it to go from rags to riches, materially and spiritually, several times already.

Now it's your turn.